WINGED WONDERS

WINGED WONDERS

A Celebration of Birds in Human History

PETER WATKINS

AND

JONATHAN STOCKLAND

BlueBridge

Jacket design by Stefan Killen Design

*Cover art by The Bridgeman Art Library (Melchior de Hondecoeter
[1636–95], Palace of Amsterdam with Exotic Birds)*

Originally published in the United Kingdom
by the Canterbury Press Norwich of
9-17 St Albans Place, London N1 0NX

Library of Congress Cataloging-in-Publication Data

Watkins, Peter, 1934-
Winged wonders : a celebration of birds in human history / Peter Watkins
and Jonathan Stockland — 1st ed.
p. cm.
ISBN 1-933346-07-8
1. Birds — History. I. Stockland, Jonathan. II. Title.
QL672.7.W38 2007
598 — dc22
2007010194

Published in North America by
B l u e B r i d g e
An imprint of
United Tribes Media Inc.
240 West 35th Street, Suite 500
New York, NY 10001
www.bluebridgebooks.com

Printed in the United States of America

10 9 8 7 6 5 4 3 2 1

Contents

Introduction   ix

  1   The Cock   1
  2   The Cuckoo   11
  3   The Dove   25
  4   The Eagle   37
  5   The Falcon   49
  6   The Goose   65
  7   The Kingfisher   83
  8   The Ostrich   87
  9   The Owl   95
 10   The Peacock   107
 11   The Pelican   121
 12   The Raven   135
 13   The Robin   143
 14   The Sparrow   153
 15   The Swan   161
 16   The Wren   173
 17   Bird Illustrators   181
 18   State Birds   187
 19   Birdsong   191

Index   202

Acknowledgments   208

We are delighted to dedicate this book to the grandchildren with whom we have been blessed: Gabriel, Konrad, Meron, Milly, Mosey, and Sophie

Introduction

Birds belong to two worlds: to our world, the earth beneath us – and to their world, the limitless skies above us. We can only truly share their soaring perspective through our imagination or, artificially, in our flying machines. They not only own the skies but enter our habitat at will, at home in countryside and city. In both worlds they are our constant and omnipresent companions, messengers of spontaneity and grace, a vivid symbol of the freedoms to which humankind aspires.

We plod our earthly way clumsy and labored, while birds rejoice in seemingly effortless flight, their movments graceful and their agility astonishing. Their speed and stamina defy distance and climate. In a flash they cross rivers and mountains and mock the walls and frontiers that humans build to keep each other in – or out. What we achieve only with hard endeavor, they accomplish with ease. They transform our world, bringing to it joy and beauty. In them we have been given gifts of grace: their dazzling

colors, the loveliness of their songs, their ingenious nest building, the fine structure of their feathers, their amazing feats of
migration – and so much more. Aristophanes exposed with
merciless prejudice the imbalance between humans and birds
in these lines from his satirical play *The Birds:*

> Ye children of Man, whose life is a span
> Protracted with sorrow from day to day,
> Naked and featherless, feeble and querulous,
> Sickly, calamitous creatures of clay;
> Attend to the words of the sovereign birds,
> Immortal, illustrious lords of the air,
> Who survey from on high with merciful eye
> Your struggles of misery, labour and care.
> Whence you may learn and clearly discern
> Such truths as attract your inquisitive turn.

Birds leave us spellbound with amazement, and touch our
hearts and raise our spirits. They immensely enrich our lives
and have done so since the beginning of recorded time.
Painted on cave walls and sculpted in bone, birds clearly fas-
cinated early humans, and were to become for us a deeply
enriching part of our sensibility. This is reflected later in language, fables, legends, and folklore; in poems and nursery
rhymes; in visual imagery and heraldry; in stories about saints
and mystics and the symbolism of the world's religions, as
well as in music and dance. *Winged Wonders* is a celebration
of some of the birds that animate our everyday lives and have
long fired human creativity.

Symbolic Birds

Legends about birds are countless. In the bestiaries of the
Middle Ages, birds also became symbols of piety. Here is a
taste of this delightful tradition.

The Stormy Petrel is one of the smallest of the web-footed birds, whose surface-skimming flight over wild oceans was thought to touch the waves as if it were walking on water. This led sailors, thinking of St. Peter walking on the storm-tossed waters of Lake Galilee, to attach to that bird the name 'Petrel,' meaning 'Little Peter,' from the Italian *petrello*. Sailors prized them as a storm-warning sign and therefore as their protectors. The bird's nickname, 'Mother Carey's Chicken,' is most likely a corruption of the Latin *Mater Cara* or 'Dear Mother,' a name for the Virgin Mary, who was regarded as the supreme protector of all humankind.

A great many of the legends involve saints and birds. Among these we find the story of St. Columba and his kindness towards a heron; that of St. Kentigern restoring life to a robin; and the story of a wren nesting in the cloak of St. Malo. Other stories tell of a blackbird nesting in St. Kevin's hand; St. Werburga and the goose; and another, of St. Hugh's friendship with a swan. Perhaps the most famous saintly tale concerning birds is that of St. Francis of Assisi, who preached to them. Born about 1181 and dying in 1226, Francis is said to have delivered this sermon to them:

O thou little Brother, that brimmest with full heart, and having naught, possessest all, surely thou dost well to sing! For thou hast life without labour, and beauty without burden, and riches without care. When thou wakest, lo, it is dawn; and when thou comest to sleep it is eve. And when

thy two wings lie folded about thy heart, lo, there is rest.
Therefore sing, Brother, having this great wealth, that when
thou singest thou givest thy riches to all.

St. Francis

In pre-Christian times the Romans, too,
regarded the presence of birds so essential to
human happiness that in describing the dark
and bleak misery of the underworld of the
dead, they called the lake entrance to it
Avernus, Greek *a-ornus*, 'without a bird' –
thus a place of ultimate cheerlessness.

Birds in Imagery and Language

References to birds abound in our vocabulary and in the most unlikely places, not least
in the world of sport. For instance, they appear in golf's
terminology: when a player sinks a putt at one under par, it is
a 'birdie'; two under par is an 'eagle'; and three under, an
'albatross.' A 'magpie' is a term in shooting for a shot
in the outermost ring but one of the target. Lightweight box-
ers are described as 'bantams,' while whole sports teams
adopt birds as their icons.

In ancient Egyptian hieroglyphics birds were used extensively to represent the visual ideograms in which that symbolic language expressed itself. And symbolic birds throng the
margins of illuminated manuscripts. We 'read' sacred paintings according to a symbolic code where images of birds are
prominent: doves signify the Holy Spirit; the goldfinch,
Christ's passion; the peacock, his resurrection. And the secu-
lar world has adopted bird imagery in heraldry and crests,
flags and emblems, on logos and trademarks, and on coins
and inn signs.

We ascribe the names of birds to people, too. We call someone who preys on the vulnerable a 'vulture.' Those advocating

warlike policies are called 'hawks,' while 'doves' are those who work for peace. To boast of one's superiority is to 'crow,' but we pity husbands who are 'henpecked.' Someone who has a 'magpie' mind is considered a chatterer or indiscriminate collector. A 'grouse' is someone who grumbles and complains, and a silly old 'coot' is a foolish person. Whereas when children play, they 'lark' about.

The collective names we have given birds over time spring from dialect and common speech and reflect the creative dynamism which their presence has brought into our lives.

The Attractive Collection

These may or may not be lexicologically correct, many are dialect forms, but nothing can rob us of the delight given by these words:

a chattering of choughs

a covert of coots

a herd of cranes

a herd of curlew

a trip of dotterel

a flight, dole, or piteous-
    ness of doves

a raft, bunch, or paddling
    of ducks on water

a team of wild ducks in
    flight

a fling of dunlins

a charm or chirm of finches

a gaggle, team, or wedge of
    geese

a skein of geese in flight

a pack or covey of grouse

a cast of hawks let fly

a siege of herons

a desert of lapwing

an exaltation or bevy of
    larks

a tiding of magpies

a plump, sord, or sute of
    mallards

a *richesse* of martins

a watch of nightingales

a parliament of owls

a covey of partridges

a muster of peacocks

a rookery of penguins

a head or (dial) nye of pheasants

a kit of pigeons flying together

a rush or flight of pochards

a covey of ptarmigan

an unkindness of ravens

a building of rooks

a wisp or walk of snipe

a host of sparrows

a murmuration of starlings

a flight of swallows

a game or herd of swans

a wedge of swans in flight

a herd of wrens

Bird Quotations

But ask the animals, and they will teach you;
the birds of the air, and they will tell you . . .

Job 12:7

Look at the birds of the air; they neither
sow nor reap nor gather into barns, and yet
your heavenly Father feeds them.

Jesus of Nazareth, Matthew 6:26a

Ubi aves, ibi angeli.
(Where there are birds, there are angels.)

Thomas Aquinas (1225–74)

And hark! How blithely the throstle sings!
He, too, is no mean preacher:
Come forth into the light of things,
Let Nature be your teacher.

William Wordsworth (1770–1850)

. . . the wise thrush; he sings each song twice over,
Lest you should think he never could recapture
The first fine careless rapture!

Robert Browning (1812–89)

I went into the woods
And built me a kirk,
And all the birds of the air
They helped me to work.

The hawk, with his long claws,
Pulled down the stone;
The dove with her rough bill,
Brought me them home.

The parrot was the clergyman,
The peacock was the clerk,
The bullfinch played the organ,
And we made merry work.

A nursery rhyme

Books! 'tis a dull and endless strife:
Come, hear the woodland linnet,
How sweet his music! on my life,
There's more of wisdom in it.

William Wordsworth (1770–1850)

. . . and heard the birds singing in that chorus of song which
can only be heard at that time of the year at dawn or at sunset. I remember now the shock of surprise with which the

sound broke on my ears. It seemed to me that I had never heard the birds singing before and I wondered whether they sang like this all the year round and I had never noticed it. . . . A lark rose suddenly from the ground beside the tree where I was standing and poured out its song above my head, and then sank still singing to rest. Everything then grew still as the sunset faded and the veil of dusk began to cover the earth. I remember now the feeling of awe which came over me. I felt inclined to kneel on the ground, as though I had been standing in the presence of an angel; and I hardly dared to look at the face of the sky, because it seemed as though it was but a veil before the face of God.

Bede Griffiths, *The Golden String*, 1954

Answer to a Child's Question

Do you ask what the birds say? The sparrow, and the dove,
The linnet and thrush say, 'I love and I love!'
In the winter they're silent – the wind is so strong;
What it says, I don't know, but it sings a loud song.
But green leaves, and blossoms, and sunny warm weather,
And singing, and loving – all come back together.
But the lark is so brimful of gladness and love,
The green fields below him, the blue sky above,
That he sings, and he sings, and forever sings he –
'I love my Love, and my Love loves me!'

Samuel Taylor Coleridge (1772–1834)

1

The Cock

The raucous abrasive crow of the cock has always been nature's alarm clock. 'The pick-axe voice of a cock, beginning to break up the night,' is how the playwright Christopher Fry describes that sound which so pierces our sleep. 'Cockcrow' is another way of saying 'the dawn,' but in fact cocks crow just before daybreak. The ancient Hebrews accurately observed this by calling the third of their four watches of the night 'the cock-crowing time.' So also the Romans called their third division of the night, at 3 a.m., *gallicinium* ('of the cocks'), and it was only the fifth that brought in the dawn itself.

In classical Greece, the cock was Apollo's bird. Apollo was the god of sun and light, and the cock announced his daily appearance. It was also associated with his son, Asclepius, the god of medicine, because of the healing properties of the sun, which also nurtured the herbs, the principal source of cures in those days. When someone was very ill, the

Greeks would sacrifice a cock, hoping thus to effect a cure. 'We owe Asclepius a cock,' said Socrates on his death-bed. 'Well, then, settle my debt, bear it in mind.' Death, to the philosopher, was the final 'cure.'

The Romans with their practical, trading acumen made the cock one of the signs of Mercury, god of commerce, because it always encouraged merchants to rise early to get to work.

But not only was it mortals who were awoken by cock-crow. In the ale-drenched Hall of Heroes, the Norse Valhalla, a golden-crested cock called the warriors to renew their drinking bouts.

Muslims tell of a cock in the heavens that sings a celestial song of morning praise to Allah, and it is this paean that cocks on earth repeat. The Prophet declared, 'The white cock is my friend; he is the enemy of the enemies of God,' who inhabit the darkness which is banished by the song of the cock.

It is, however, as the master of courtesy that the cock is seen in the Talmud, the authoritative collection of Jewish teaching, because each day he loudly ushers in his Lord the Sun.

The Fighting Cock

If you were ever to walk into a chicken run, with a 'cock o' the roost' in charge, you would be in no doubt as to its bravery and fierceness. 'Cockily' strutting towards you, clucking threateningly, comb ablaze, tail feathers waving, the rooster is the very picture of the doughty guardian, the noisy, top fowl of the farmyard. John Milton, in his poem 'Allegro,' captures its essence:

> While the cock with lively din
> Scatters the rear of darkness thin,
> And to the stack or barn door,
> Stoutly struts his dames before.
>
> John Milton (1608–74)

It was for these combative qualities, not as a food source, that our cock's ancestor, *Gallus gallus*, the red jungle fowl of North India, was first captured and bred around 2500 BCE. 'To live like a fighting cock' was to enjoy the best of food and care, albeit in a tough training regimen, so that your fighting performance would be enhanced.

However, purity of lineage was the basic guarantee of the cock's fighting prowess. If there was any hint of inferior or unsupervised breeding, such as a white feather in its plumage, the cock became suspect. Thus 'to show a white feather' was a sign of cowardice and an unwillingness to fight.

Such was the cock's reputation that medieval bestiaries (books of animal facts and figures, stories and legends) claimed even the lion was afraid of it, especially of the pure white variety – a sudden reversal of color symbolism.

So today, the cock is still an emblem of courage: we find it in the sport of boxing in the word 'bantamweight,' which signifies a fighter weighing between 51 and 54 kilos (112 and 119 lbs.), and so one of the lightest pugilists. It derives from the word 'bantam,' a small feisty fowl, originally from the Indonesian island of Java.

At the other end of the scale is the White Sully, a Californian fowl, which produces 'roosters' weighing up to 22 lbs., and is extremely aggressive. One such bird is known to have killed two cats and crippled a dog. Its name was 'Weirdo.'

The cock also became, after the French Revolution of 1789, the national emblem of France, *le coq gaulois*. The Latin word *gallus*, meaning both 'cock' and 'Gaul' (the old word for the French), was an irresistible combination for the Paris revolutionaries who had won such an unlikely political battle.

The sight of *le coq* on an international rugby football field, before a match between England and France, is guaranteed to inflame English fans and inspire their French counterparts, perhaps making the latter 'cock-a-hoop,' supremely confident, from the French word *huppe* or erect crest, or, possibly, 'cocksure,' with its reference to the tap on a barrel of beer and the false or 'Dutch' courage that alcohol produces. But 'cock-sure' could also mean having a sure trust in God, as used by John Foxe in his famous *Book of Martyrs* published in 1563: 'Whoso dwelleth under . . . the help of the Lord, shall be cock-sure for evermore.'

The Weathercock

The vigilant song of the cock signaled the end of darkness and the beginning of the light. The night of our ancestors was full of real and imagined fears, a time for ghosts and unclean spirits to roam abroad, a place where the forces of good and evil struggled together. As the cock was the herald of the dawn, when darkness was dispelled, people came to believe that he was the instrument itself by which good prevailed. In Shakespeare's *Hamlet*, the ghost of Hamlet's father has been seen on the battlements of Elsinore castle. But then, reports one of the sentries,

> The cock crew loud
> And at the sound, it [the ghost] shrunk in haste away
> And vanished from our sight.

An old country saying offers further proof of the cock as ghost buster: 'Keep a dog to drive off humans, a cock to drive off ghosts and your stock will thrive.' With another making even larger claims: 'A cock will frighten away the devil himself, so set it on weathervanes and churches to face the four ways that the wind blows.'

So came the weathercock. Set on the highest point of the church, like an all-seeing eye, turning as the wind of the Spirit directed, it acted as a 'scare-devil.' Its role was deepened by the gospel story of the cock whose crowing signaled St. Peter's denial of his Master:

And the second time the cock crew. And Peter called to mind the word that Jesus said unto him, Before the cock crow twice, thou shalt deny me thrice.

Mark 14:72

So the weathercock became a sign of the Christian's vigilance against sin and against betrayal of Christian vows and obedience.

In France, legend gave rise to another somewhat crueler interpretation: that St. Peter, angry with the cock because it had reminded him of his cowardice, impaled it on a spike and set it on high for all men to see.

In actual fact, the first weathercock was probably mounted at Brescia in Italy around 800 CE.

In Norse mythology, the cock sat on the topmost branches of the eternal, cosmic ash tree Yggdrasil, also as a vigilant watchman, to give early warning to the gods of any attack by their enemies, the giants.

Cockfighting

If not quite the sport of kings, pitting cock against cock was an adversarial pastime of worldwide popularity from earliest times. The 'cockpit' or arena was a circular space in any village or town street; ownership did not require vast sums of money, the rules were simple, and betting was one of the prime attractions.

The sport was considered a manly practice in the classical era of Greece and Rome. Before the Battle of Marathon in 490 BCE, Militiades, the Athenian commander in chief, ordered cockfights to be staged before all his troops. He intended the fierce bravery of the cocks to instill courage into his soldiers and arouse their aggression. It worked. Despite being outnumbered, the Greeks won a notable victory over the Persians through sheer tenacity and courage. Their feat of arms became part of human sporting history, too, because news of the battle's outcome was taken to Athens straight from the battlefield by a single runner who, having run the 26 miles and delivered his message, fell dead at the citizens' feet. Henceforth the 'marathon' race was incorporated in the Olympic Games in commemoration of this.

In Britain, cockfighting flourished from the Middle Ages onwards. Despite attempts by the Puritans to ban it, it was finally outlawed only in 1855. Royalty patronized the cockpit at London's Whitehall, although they had their own royal cockpit in nearby Birdcage Walk, set among the cages of exotic birds spilling over from the Royal Menagerie in St. James's Park. Meetings could last for days; vast sums changed hands; hundreds of birds were killed. In 1607, King James was made 'very merry' at Lincoln by the spectacle of a 'battle royal,' a contest in which great numbers of cocks were pitted against one another until only the supreme victor remained standing.

To shorten the duration of the fights, steel spurs were strapped to the birds' feet, a reminder of which can be seen in the emblem of a London association football club, Tottenham Hotspur, which is a white cock with spurs on its feet.

Until the nineteenth century, it was an approved annual sport in some private schools, traditionally taking place on Shrove Tuesday. A schoolmaster collected a tax from the schoolboys taking part; indeed, in Scotland it is a matter of record that the income of one such 'beak' was made up of salary, fees, and cockfight dues.

Throwing sticks and stones at a tethered cock was another barbaric Shrove Tuesday practice – 'cock shy,' meaning a 'free throw,' derives from this.

Chanticleer

This name for a cock is adapted from the French *chanter clair*, 'to sing clearly.' He first appears, together with his hen consort Partlet or Pertelote, in 1200 CE in an anonymous medieval collection of tales, *Roman de Renart*, 'The Story of Reynard [the fox].'

In the fourteenth century, Geoffrey Chaucer based his 'Nun's Priest's Tale' on the same three characters, focusing on the cock's pride in his vainglorious crowing and the hen's silliness. Their folly enables Reynard to carry off Chanticleer, until the cock turns the tables by so flattering the fox that Chanticleer manages to escape to the safety of a tree.

This boastful reputation permanently attached itself to the cock in its guise as Chanticleer. In George Eliot's *Adam Bede* (1859), we find Mrs. Poyser, the tart farmer's wife, remarking sarcastically of a gardener she dislikes, 'I think he's welly [very] like a cock, as thinks the sun's rose o' purpose to hear him crow.' And Edmond Rostand's satirical play *Chantecler* emphasizes this aspect in these damning lines:

> Je recule
> Ebloui de me voir moi même tout vermeil
> Et d'avoir, moi, le coq, fait élèver le soleil.
> (I step back, dazzled to see myself all over vermilion
> And having, myself, the cock, made the sun to rise.)
> Edmond Rostand (1868–1918)

The Cock of Compostela

Traditionally, the body of the Apostle St. James the Greater was believed to be buried at a small town in northern Spain called Compostela. Hence Santiago (St. James) de Compostela became a favored place of pilgrimage for all Europe, and a center for resistance to the Muslim invasions from North Africa from 711 onwards. Miracles and legends grew up around the site and none more vivid than the following.

A young lad on pilgrimage rebuffed the advances of a girl in the inn where he was staying. She revenged herself by framing him for the theft of a goblet for which crime the punishment was death by hanging. He was duly hanged. But his parents, coming to claim his body, visited the shrine, where they heard his voice telling them that he was alive. Amazed, they requested audience of the *corregidor* (local governor), who scornfully told them that their son was as dead as the roast cock and hen he was about to eat on his plate. At which point, the fowls leapt up in the air and crowed!

Since that time a live cock and hen, always white, are kept in the cathedral and are said to be offered, under an indulgence of 1350 signed by 180 bishops, to all who devoutly walk round the tomb reciting 'Our Father,' 'Hail Mary,' and 'Gloria.'

The Word of God

A delightful legend tells that it was the cock who first announced the birth of Christ. It happened in this way: on the night of his nativity, Jesus came to earth as the Word of all creation, so that all his creatures, all birds and beasts, could share with him in the work of salvation. To do this they were blessed with speech (albeit only Latin!) so that they, too, could tell out the good news. The cock as the announcer of the break of day cried out first, '*Christus natus est,*' 'Christ is born.' Then the goose and crow, and the owl and the lamb, sounding very much like themselves, joined in. '*Quando? Quando?*' 'When? When?' queried the goose. '*In hac nocte,*' 'In this night,' croaked the crow. '*Ubi? Ubi?*' hooted the owl, 'Where? Where?' to which the lamb answered with the bleat '*Be-e-e-ethlehem.*'

It is also said that ever after the Nativity cocks would crow-talk throughout the night of Christmas Eve, and every bird and beast joined in.

This poem from the age of Shakespeare, in which a perpetual pun is put on the words 'Sun' and 'Son,' shows the connection between the light of day and the light Jesus Christ brings into the world:

Chanticleer

All this night shrill chanticleer,
Day's proclaiming trumpeter,
Claps his wings and loudly cries,
See a wonder
Heaven is under;
From the earth is risen a Sun
Shines all night, though day be done.

Wake, O earth, wake everything!
Wake and hear the joy I bring;
Wake and joy; for all this night
Heaven and every twinkling light,
All amazing
Still stand gazing.
Angels, Powers, and all that be,
Wake, and joy this Sun to see.

Hail, O Sun, O blessed Light,
Sent into the world by night!
Let thy rays and heavenly powers
Shine in these dark souls of ours;
For most duly
Thou art truly
God and man, we do confess:
Hail, O Sun of Righteousness.

William Austin (1587–1634)

The Inner Bird

As Apollo's chosen bird, the cock had another, more macabre role: to provide its corpse for divination. The diviner, whose findings were taken with great seriousness by great and poor alike, would cut open the fowl and 'read' its entrails which it seems were particularly easy to interpret. In a later era, that exposer of superstition, Pliny, the Roman naturalist, slightingly remarked that an insignificant and dead cock could hold sway over governments.

Hens also lent themselves to the prophetic art but by a more humane method: placed in a large cage they were offered food. If they ate it greedily the omens were good; if not, the outlook was poor. There seems little doubt that it was a method open to manipulation. The military used it for its convenience, but a Roman general, once thwarted in his efforts to stack the odds, threw the cage into the sea with the remark, 'Let them drink if they won't eat.' His subsequent defeat was blamed entirely on his misconduct with the hens.

The Chinese ideograms (written symbols) for good or favorable omen and that for cock are homophonic, being pronounced *ki*, so that in China the cock is regarded as having a benign influence. It is also one of the 12 animals that are part of the Chinese zodiac.

2

The Cuckoo

Why was the cuckoo ever made?
Did the Creator, all plans laid
For a perfect world, draw back in doubt,
Feeling the need for a layabout?
For creatures artful and worldly-wise
To walk the earth or skim the skies
And give to life an abrasive touch,
Lest a perfect world be just too much?
Profligate parent, carefree cad,
Sign that the earth is for good and bad –
Welcome cuckoo! – I have no doubt
The good Lord knows what He's about.

Edith Simpson, *It Takes All Sorts*

Members of the cuckoo family are found worldwide, and although less than half are parasitical, most have their own odd quirks of behavior. The Roadrunner of North America seldom takes to the air, but prefers to try to outrun its enemies and seize 'on the hoof' its prey of snakes, including rattle-snakes, scorpi-ons, and other smaller reptiles. The Black- and Yellow-billed Cuckoos are known as 'rain-crows' as they vociferously cry 'kuk-kuk-kuk' before summer storms. To add to the disruptions, their off-spring can climb when ten days old, which makes for an exceptionally rambunctious as well as noisy nest life. The Hawk Cuckoo of the Indian subcontinent also heralds approaching storms with a loud screaming call – it sounds like 'brain fever, brain fever' and is repeated all day long.

In Central America, the Squirrel Cuckoo seems to have a merely residual memory of nest building, and has been observed trying unsuccessfully to balance leaves and sticks on a mango tree onto which it deposits an egg that instantly falls to the ground and smashes. Definitely cuckoo!

The European cuckoo has received a mixed reception since biblical times. In Hebrew law it was linked with scavengers and raptors, such as the vulture and owl, as a creature to be 'held in abomination,' but whether this prohibition was the result of its habits or its reputation in surrounding religious cultures is unclear. No doubt it would have seemed a strange bird with its singular, ventriloquist's call (soft yet penetrating and insistent), its sudden appearance in spring and conse-quent disappearance in late summer, its general elusiveness, and its apparent lack of any natural feeling towards its young. All these characteristics gave rise to intense interest and con-jecture, among poets as among ordinary country people, and have given birth to fable and folklore.

The Odd Man Out

The cuckoo is a bird of extraordinary habits, of amazing wiles and ruses. It is, in our terms, a rebel and even a renegade. It is no wonder that we call people 'cuckoo' when they depart from what is generally considered to be normal behavior.

The list of crimes and misdemeanors brought against the

common European species (*Cuculus canoris*) is as follows: it does not build its own nest, but deposits its eggs in the nest of another bird; it does not incubate its eggs; it does not feed its young nor does it rear them. If this were not enough, the cuckoo is polyandrous – that is, the female mates with more than one male, an occurrence in only one percent of all bird species. Even its feeding habits are abnormal with a penchant for huge, hairy, highly colored caterpillars that are poisonous to most other birds. And yet despite what seems like grave dereliction of duty and decidedly nasty habits, the cuckoo is held in great affection.

Ornithological studies increase our amazement at the cuckoo's adaptive devices and the thoroughness of deception involved in its brood parasitism, although not all species of cuckoo are such parasites. Studies have shown the female spying out the potential nests of other birds, lurking in the vicinity with malice aforethought until the exact moment when the hard-working parents have completed their building work and begun to lay their brood of eggs. This activity stimulates our cuckoo into getting her own eggs ready for delivery and, with perfect timing, she swoops down upon the selected site, grips the rim of it with her specially designed claws, seizes one of the existing eggs in her beak, which she will later eat or just discard on the ground, and then deposits her own egg in its place. In the English county of Northamptonshire, she is called 'the suckegg' and it is believed she can only sing once she has consumed an egg! This masterpiece of deception is in fact swift, silent, and systematic; the egg drop lasts little more than ten seconds. And the cuckoo, after only 24 hours or more, will repeat the process in another nest until she has successfully scattered some dozen eggs in the nests of a dozen unsuspecting foster parents.

But the mastery is in the thoroughness of the deception. Cuckoo eggs are the same color as the host bird's but a little larger, so that they appear slightly superior to those they are mimicking. They are also noticeably denser in order to survive their hurried entry and the crowded conditions of the nest. The cuckoo's eggs will hatch earlier, too, to their great advantage, because the embryo has already been developed in the egg duct before being laid. Thus the cuckoo enjoys more than a head start on its fellow fledglings.

The Young Delinquent

Just a few hours after hatching, the interloper sets about ridding itself of all competition. When it comes into contact with another egg, it maneuvers the egg to the side of the nest and with immense effort tips it over the edge, repeating this until it has sole occupancy.

Once it has eliminated or severely limited the competition, the young cuckoo demands the undivided attention of its unwitting foster parents who are worn to a shred trying to cope with the appetite of their one giant child of forced adoption. They find out what it really means 'to have a cuckoo in the nest.' Dunnocks, Reed Warblers, and Meadow Pipits are the most usual host choices, although cuckoo eggs have been found in the nests of about 50 different species. The choice of nest proves at times the wily cuckoo's undoing, for it can outgrow its colonized domain, collapsing it and, in the case of the Reed Warbler, falling to a watery grave or, with the wren, bursting clear through the dome. There is a short 'nonsense' poem by E. Lucia Turnbull that anticipates the worst:

'My dear', said Mrs Wren, 'If Mrs Cuckoo comes to call,
I really think it would be best to see her in the hall,
Explaining that our house is so very, very small
We have no room for paying guests, or any guests at all.'

The young cuckoo has an insistent cry, which both for volume and frequency is the equal of a full complement of nestlings, along with a wide red gape of its open beak with distinct inside markings, both of which act as an intense stimulant for its adoptive parents to meet its requirements. This they do in a frenzy of food collection of insects for body-building protein. It is also known but remains unexplained that, oddly, young cuckoos, who have flown the nest and yet remain dependent, can still persuade birds with no relation to them at all to meet their food needs! The relative sizes of hosts to cuckoo chick are sometimes so unequal that the host parent is forced to perch on the young cuckoo's back in order to feed it, and the adult bird seems almost to disappear down the youngster's gaping maw. This is probably the source of the misconception that the young cuckoo swallows its host.

A Cuckoo Legend

There is a legendary explanation as to why the European cuckoo adopted its distinctive lifestyle. The legend has it that at the holy festival of the Virgin Mary all the birds ceased work in order to venerate her, except the cuckoo – who just kept building her nest. As a punishment, she has never been allowed to build another one and therefore has to wander the earth alone, forever denied any form of domestic bliss. A more scientific conclusion would be that having 'discovered' brood parasitism (the use of others to rear one's own offspring), the cuckoo realized its advantages for its own species' survival and genetically passed this advantage down. But how and why the brood parasitism first came about remains a mystery.

Another mystery is how the cuckoo young learn to migrate. We know the parent birds migrate in August at the latest, yet the young leave far later in the autumn. So how do they know to migrate or where to go? Is it wholly from genetic imprinting? A case of nature over nurture?

The Harbinger of Spring

Summer is icumen in,
Loude sing cuccu!
Spryngeth sed and bloweth mede
And groweth the wude nu.

English song, ca. 1250

So closely is the appearance of the cuckoo associated with the coming of spring that in the West Country, in England, the cuckoo was said 'to eat up the dirt' because its spring arrival coincided with good weather making the lanes and streets free of mud. So regular was its appearance that the Greek historian Hesiod advised farmers to plow the fields when they heard the cuckoo sing in the oak trees. Classical myth, too, associated the bird with spring, for Hera, goddess of fertility, was, in one legend, seduced by Zeus on Mount Kokkygia by his fluttering into her bosom in the guise of a storm-driven cuckoo, or, by interpretation, Zeus created spring through the good offices of the cuckoo!

Then there is the twinned tradition of the April fool on the first day of April and 'hunting the gowk.' *Gowk* is Icelandic for cuckoo and is still used in Scotland to this day. *Gowk* is also Teutonic for fool and from this we get the adjective 'gawky,' meaning awkward or clumsy, and its French derivative *gauche*, meaning unsophisticated. Both cuckoo and fool come together on the first day of April when people play silly tricks on one another or send the unsuspecting on false errands. We may be able to trace the origins of April Fool's Day to the Roman festival of Cerealia, which in early April celebrated the arrival of spring. Cerealia was linked to Pluto, god of the underworld, who in springtime spirited Proserpina down to Hades, still bearing in her lap an apron of daffodils. When her mother, Ceres, heard her screams, she searched frantically but in vain for her daughter, following the voice but never finding its owner. This is often the case when we try to locate the cuckoo: the call is clear but its source elusive – we, too, thus find ourselves on a fool's errand.

The Cuckoo Call

The cuckoo arrives in Britain in early April from its winter quarters in Africa. The male cuckoo's distinctive call of two notes is easily recognizable and is repeated over and over again when it arrives in its territory. A. E. Housman referred to the cuckoo who 'shouts all day at nothing.' First sightings of its arrival or hearing its call are of such public interest that letters to *The Times* newspaper on the subject have become a national institution, probably because it is often difficult to tell from the weather whether spring has arrived or not! Traditionally much folklore was attached to 'cuckoo-day': turning the money in your pocket meant riches in the coming year ('cuckoos' was slang for money in the seventeenth century). It was also said to be the moment to make the wish nearest to your heart, and traditions dating back to Roman times advised lovers that on hearing the first cuckoo in spring they should search for a hair under their feet because this hair's color would foretell that of their future spouse. This legend seems to have survived at least to the seventeenth century in England, for in an edition of *Mother Bunch's Closet* (1685) we read:

> The first time you hear a cuckoo sing look under your left shoe and you will find a hair the colour of your wife or husband, without the help of the Devil.

Folklore also instructed adherents to count the number of cuckoo calls in succession in order to work out how soon they would marry, how many children they would have, or when they would die, whichever was the most applicable! This lore may have prompted the Danes to deduce that the reason the cuckoo had no time to build a nest was that it was too busy answering people's questions!

The familiar notes of the male cuckoo are heard only during its short breeding season. Afterwards it tails off. Later the 'bubbling' song of the female is more in evidence. An old rhyme charts the bird's progress through spring and summer, but makes the mistake of implying that the male does all the singing:

> In April come he will
> In May he sings all day
> In June he changes his tune
> In July he prepares to fly
> In August go he must.

Old rhymes also advised farmers to synchronize various seasonal jobs on the land with the cuckoo's comings and goings:

> When cuckoo doth sing upon the green bough,
> Then into the earth let enter your plough.

Or:
> Cuckoo oats and woodcock hay
> Make a farmer run away.

(Which means that if the farmer sows his oats too early in April, or reaps too late, by the time Woodcock shooting begins in November, he will be ruined.)

And:

> When the cuckoo comes to the bare thorn,
> Sell your cow and buy your corn;

But when she comes to the full bit,
Sell your corn and buy your sheep.

The Adulterous Cuckoo

It was thought that the cuckoo's heartless exploitation of the family life of others, and the way in which it casually abandoned its young, was evidence enough to conclude that it was also an adulterer. The Romans called an adulterer a cuckoo, as we read in Plautus's *Asinaria*, whereas in Britain the 'cuckold' was the one sinned against: the husband of the wayward wife. Near Deptford on the Thameside is Cuckold's Point. It is so called from a tradition that King John made love to a laborer's wife there. Early English usage described a shrewish woman as a *cuck* or *scold*, suggesting that the injured husband suffered both the adultery and his wife's ridicule. There is also a tenuous connection with the Greek *kuk-kuk*, meaning 'Where? Where?'– the directionless discomfiture of a poor husband searching for his erring wife. Shakespeare, in *Love's Labor's Lost*, has lines that echo this:

> The cuckoo then on every tree
> Mocks married men, for thus sings he,
> Cuckoo
> O, note of fear,
> Unpleasing to the married ear.

In France they even had 'cuckoo courts,' in which husbands deceived by their wives could appear, perhaps to noise abroad their grievances and obtain compensation from the guilty parties. The Old French word *coucou* from the sixteenth century signified both cuckoo and cuckold. The following rhymes – in English – reflect the *double entendre*.

Cuckoos lead Bohemian lives,
They fail as husbands and as wives,
As so they cynically disparage
Everybody else's marriage.

Anonymous

When Pontius wished an edict might be passed
That cuckolds should into the sea be cast,
His wife, assenting, thus replied to him,
'But first, my dear, I'd have ye learn to swim.'

Source unknown, possibly Matthew Prior

The Cuckoo Clock

The word *coucou*, French for 'cowslip,' is also the French word for 'cuckoo clock.' People often make the mistake of associating this clock exclusively with Switzerland. In fact, it probably owes its creation in the eighteenth century to the clock maker Franz Anton Ketterer of Schönwald in Germany's Black Forest. Subsequently, an enormous number of cuckoo clocks were produced, first in Germany, then elsewhere. The hours (and half-hours) are marked by a wooden cuckoo popping out to announce the time with its traditional call 'Cuckoo! Cuckoo!' A song in the *Sound of Music* uses the cuckoo's call to signal bedtime for the Von Trapp children.

The birdcage clock also became very popular in the eighteenth century; the base of the cage contained the clock and, on the hour, the mechanical bird inside the cage fluttered its wings and turned its head from side to side. It opened its beak and sang a song, which was produced by air blown through a reed or whistle.

Cloud-Cuckoo-Land

If someone is indulging in an absurdly over-optimistic fantasy or is making an impractical or utopian plan, we say that they are living in 'cloud-cuckoo-land.' The expression comes from *The Birds*, a comedy by the Greek dramatist Aristophanes, who lived between about 450 and about 380 BCE. He is thought to have written some 40 plays, but only 11 have survived intact. In this comedy the birds build an imaginary capital city in the air which they call Nephelokokkygia – a name made up from the Greek words for cloud, *nephelě*, and for cuckoo, *kokkux*.

Insects and Flowers

Cuckoo spit is the white froth found on plant stems and leaves – it encloses and protects the larvae of the spit bug or froghopper, a jumping frog-like bug. It was once believed to be the sputum of the cuckoo itself, probably because the appearance of cuckoo and cuckoo spit was more or less simultaneous.

The ruby-tailed wasp is also called the cuckoo wasp because some species lay eggs in the nests of the solitary wasps and bees in a way analogous to that in which some cuckoos lay eggs in the nests of other birds. The cuckoo wasp larva either eats the other larva or starves it to death by devouring all the food.

Country folk were not slow to think up tales that linked the season and creatures: they claimed there was 'an irreconcilable hatred between Cuckoos and Grasshoppers, for it is written that Cuckoos kill them until the Dog Star arises, but afterwards the Grasshoppers creep under the wings of the Cuckoos in great numbers and bite them to death.' The Dog Star (Sirius) is visible in July and the first half of August, so here we have yet another theory as to why cuckoos disappear in midsummer. The writers of bestiaries contributed to the misinformation: 'Out of the Cuckoo spittle are Grasshoppers begotten.'

The Cuckoo Flower or Lady's Smock is a member of the mustard family which blooms from about the time the cuckoo arrives until the male bird stops singing in June. Possibly from its association with the cuckoo, it was considered an unlucky flower and was deliberately not included in the garlands that children carried in the May Day processions.

One of the best known of the British wildflowers is the Cuckoo Pint, which appears in April. This white Arum with its open hood (spathe) emits a nasty smell of rotting carrion; it does this to trap flies which it then digests for pollination purposes – a ruse worthy of the cuckoo itself. The flower is also called Jack-in-the-Pulpit from its resemblance to a preacher within a hooded pulpit.

Several other flower and plant names are associated with the cuckoo, including Cuckoo's Joy (Marsh Marigold), Cuckoo's Sorrow (Sheep's Sorrel), Cuckoo-grass (Woodrush), Cuckoo's Potatoes (Pignut), and Cuckoo's Sorrel (Wood Sorrel).

Good Tidings

The country child and the young poet reflect on the cuckoo's arrival:

> The cuckoo's a fine bird,
> He sings as he flies;
> He brings us good tidings,
> He tells us no lies.

He sucks little birds' eggs,
To make his voice clear;
And when he sings cuckoo!
The summer is near.

A nursery rhyme

The Cuckoo

Thrice welcome, darling of the spring!
Even yet thou art to me
No bird, but an invisible thing,
A voice, a mystery.

The same whom in my schoolboy days
I listened to; that cry
Which made me look a thousand ways
In bush, and tree, and sky.

To seek thee did I often rove
Through woods and on the green;
And thou wert still a hope, a love;
Still longed for, never seen.

William Wordsworth (1770–1850)

3

The Dove

And I said, Oh that I had wings like a dove!
For then I would fly away, and be at rest.

Psalm 55:6

The psalmist used the dove to express his desire for transcendence and tranquility, his spiritual aspiration and his longing to find inner peace. From this text Mendelssohn took inspiration and composed a haunting high-noted anthem conveying a yearning that soars up to heaven: 'O for the wings of a dove!'

Dove is the name for any of various birds of the family *Columbidae*. A probable derivation of the word 'dove' is from the Middle English *dufan*, to dip or dive. The male has a lavish, bobbing dance of courtship before his intended. 'Dove' is a word we love. It speaks of the bird's devotion to its young and the gentle sound of cooing. It is symbolic of peace. Pablo Picasso produced an iconic dove, a sign of many peace campaigns. The artist even named his daughter Paloma (Spanish for dove) after his pet bird.

A pigeon is a dove by any other name. It is a further example of Norman words introduced into the existing language when they described cooked birds or beasts for the table. We have pigeon pies, not dove pies. Pigeon comes from Old French *pijon*, young dove, coming from *pipio*, young bird, from *pipire*, to chirp. The cheeping came from young birds tender enough to be eaten.

Our use of the two words reveals an ambivalent attitude to the same bird. When we malign it we call it a pigeon, not a dove. It is pigeons who defecate everywhere and have to be discouraged from gathering in public places. Pigeons are attacked in proverbs: 'Pigeons and priests make foul houses.' Chaucer, in *The Canterbury Tales*, made use of this proverbial lore. Priests, he warned, invited into a household to educate the children, seduce and debauch the maids.

Our vocabulary follows this pattern. A 'pigeon' in slang is a dupe or a victim. A 'stool pigeon' is an informer to the police. To be timid or to lack courage is to be 'pigeon-hearted' or 'pigeon-livered.' Two human flaws are said to be being 'pigeon-breasted' and 'pigeon-toed': the first is an abnormal distortion of the breastbone, caused by rickets or by obstructed breathing in infancy; and the second is to have one's feet pointing inwards.

Nevertheless, the pigeon or dove is our oldest feathered friend. The Rock Pigeon has lived with humans for at least 12,000 years, and the earliest midden heaps contain pigeon bones. In Egypt, Rameses II claimed to have sacrificed 58,810 pigeons to the god Ammon at Thebes. It is clear that by 1200 BCE the Egyptians were practicing pigeon husbandry, and this husbandry continues to this day and around the world.

The Love Bird

It is remarkable that such a small creature as the dove, so modest in voice, appearance, and habits, should represent humankind's greatest passion and virtue – that of love. It might be thought that the swan, for instance, fits the role more appropriately with its white beauty and gracefulness of body movement, intense pride in and loyalty to its mate and offspring, and its awesome protective presence on lake or river.

It is the dove's extraordinary fertile power of regeneration that gives it pride of place in love's hierarchy: although it lays only two eggs at a time, it does so nine or ten times a year! Our forebears prized this assurance of family succession above all else. In ancient Egypt the bird was venerated and the *kv* sign in the sacred hieroglyphic script represents the dove. In Crete, the goddess of love and marriage, Rhea, is often portrayed with a black dove in one hand for sustained succession and, in the other, a porpoise representing sea trade, the island's life-blood. Later, Astarte from Phoenicia, and her Greek and Roman counterparts, Aphrodite and Venus, all had the dove as their symbol of love, accompanying their warriors into battle and their priests to the altar. In Hinduism the dove was also reverenced for its fertility and gentleness, and was allowed, together with the monkey and the cow, to colonize temples without restraint.

Perhaps an echo of these ancient beliefs persists in present-day Morocco, where two stuffed pigeons in an onion sauce, with lemon and honey, are served to young Jewish couples on their wedding day to wish them a sweet life full of love. The dish is called El Hamam del Aroussa, 'The Bride's Pigeons.'

The Song of Solomon poetically declares:

> How beautiful you are, my love, how very beautiful!
> Your eyes are doves behind your veil.
>
> The Song of Solomon 4:1

One of John Heath Stubbs's poems has Noah's dove not wanting to rove, but to settle down and build a nest with 'her love – the other turtle dove.' Noah knew that the flood was over because the dove, a home lover, was not a rover. Love's intensity was conveyed in William Shakespeare's *As You Like It* when Rosalind (in disguise) says to Orlando, 'I will be more jealous of thee than a Barbary cock-pigeon over his hen. . . .'

The Sacrificial Dove

The dove's reproductive energy and its religious associations had an inevitable outcome: it became a popular bird for temple sacrifice. The constant ease of its procreation matched by its docile temperament allowed it to be reared cheaply on the temple premises, thus an affordable offering for even the poorest of people and penitents. It is laid down in the Old Testament Law with a detailed prescription that seems callous to our present-day sensibilities:

> If a man's offering to the Lord is a whole-offering of birds, he shall present turtle-doves or young pigeons as his offering. The priest shall present it at the altar, and shall wrench off the head and burn it on the altar; and the blood shall be drained out against the side of the altar. He shall take away the crop and its contents in one piece, and throw it to the east side where the ashes are. He shall tear it by its wings without severing them completely, and shall burn it on the altar, on top of the wood of the altar-fire; it is a whole-offering, a food-offering of soothing odour to the Lord.
>
> Leviticus 1:14–17

Sacrifice is fundamentally an offering to God of a gift. This feature was widespread in many religions, including Judaism. In the New Testament Jesus appeared to tolerate the practice of sacrifice, but quoted with approval the teaching of Hosea placing mercy before sacrifice.

Mary and Joseph brought to the temple two doves with which to give thanks for the birth of their son Jesus. They were too poor to afford anything else more costly. Years later, Jesus violently threw over the stalls of the traders selling doves, in protest at such commercial use of the sacred precincts and the exploitation of observant pilgrims on the site.

The Medicinal Pigeon

A folklore remedy involved cutting a live pigeon in half and applying it to a sick person's body. It was believed that this would draw out the illness. Samuel Pepys twice mentioned this procedure: 'They did lay pigeons at his feet while I was in the house; and all despair left him. . . .'

The Dove and Death

The dove in folklore has also been linked with death. P. J. Kavanagh, in *Finding Connections*, mentioned a rebellion in 1798 in which 640 Irishmen were killed. He wrote this extraordinary passage:

A mother had three sons killed there that night. She didn't know they were there, didn't know where they were. Then a dove came in through the window and landed on her kitchen table and she knew they were dead. So when they were all covered over, she planted three trees there, with a spoon.

An equally extraordinary anecdote comes from John Aubrey. There was a saying, 'He who is sprinkled with pigeons' blood will never die a natural death.' Aubrey related erroneously how King Charles I was receiving a new bust of himself, sculpted by Bernini. A pigeon flew overhead and was attacked by a hawk. Blood from the pigeon fell on the bust and stained it around the neck. The stain could not be removed. Charles was beheaded on January 30, 1649, outside Whitehall Palace.

Pigeon Post

The dove's homing instinct is most famously recounted in the story of Noah and his ark in Genesis, chapter 6. Noah's dove provided the first messenger service – the prototype carrier pigeon. Three times Noah sent it out to see if the floods were subsiding. From the first foray it returned empty-beaked, the second time it returned bearing a leaf from an olive tree, indicating that the tops of the trees were emerging from the waters; sent out a third time, the dove did not return, for the waters had receded and it could seek out its own nest.

Pliny the Elder told of pigeons at the siege of Mutina in 43 BCE where Decimus Brutus sent them out with dispatches tied to their legs, and then goes on to summarize their advantages. What use to Antony were his rampart and watchful besieging force, and even nets stretched across the river, when the messenger traveled through the sky?

In 1146 CE the Caliph of Baghdad, Sultan Nuruddin, set up a nationwide winged mail service. Genghis Khan, who lived between about 1162 and 1227, used pigeon post to communicate across his vast conquests from the Black Sea to the Pacific. Pigeons were used extensively during the French Revolution. And the duke of Wellington owned a carrier pigeon that flew 5,000 miles and dropped dead from exhaustion just one mile from home.

During World War I the U.S. Army trained homing pigeons to fly by night, when they were unlikely to be attacked by birds of prey. No one knows, however, how they found their way home under moonless and overcast skies. During World War II it is estimated that some 200,000 carrier pigeons died on active service. Some stories had happy endings, though. Paddy from Northern Ireland was the first bird to come back with the good news of the Normandy landings on D-Day in 1944, relaying his message in just five hours. Then there was Cher Ami, a blue-checkered American pigeon, who flew no fewer than 12 successful sorties, with no failures.

The last courier pigeon service was disbanded in 2002: in India, Orissa State police at last conceded that mobile phones are more reliable and effective than their 1,400 highly trained birds. They were returned to the wild.

The Dove Song Contest

In Southeast Asia, from Thailand to Indonesia to Singapore, the Turtle Dove has achieved artistic fame and generated fortunes too. The Jawi, a Muslim Thai tribe, have so skilfully bred it for its song that a champion bird can cost over $50,000; so highly is it prized that its egg alone can be worth as much as $1,500. Song contests are held throughout the region. As many as 2,500 birds at a time are hung in elaborate cages draped in silk by carved ivory hooks on 23-feet-high poles, while judges walk among them assessing their songs. Once the prizes are awarded, some owners auction their birds to feather their own nests.

However, some Jawi prize their birds too highly to sell them; spurning this source of instant wealth, they bask in the sheer prestige they bring to them as owners. Their definition of bliss is to have a *kris* (a wavy bladed dagger), a good wife, a large house, and, of course, a Turtle Dove that sings.

The Passenger Pigeon

In the afternoon of September 1, 1914, a female Passenger Pigeon named Martha died in the Cincinnati Zoo – she was the last of her species. Once one of our most abundant birds, it became extinct because of human exploitation.

The North American Passenger Pigeon was first sighted in 1534 on the banks of the St. Lawrence River by the French explorer Jacques Cartier. In 1813, John Audubon noted their teeming abundance in Kentucky when a vast flock of these pigeons took over a day to pass continuously through the area, a cloud of birds a mile wide and up to 300 miles long. This flock was calculated to be a billion birds strong. But Audubon had also seen schooners along the Hudson River laden with slaughtered pigeons. They were sold for one cent a piece. Records from 1878 show that one professional hunter alone shipped three million pigeons to the market.

Audubon wrote prophetically about the Passenger Pigeon: 'When an individual is seen gliding through the woods and close to the observer, it passes like a thought, and on trying to see it again, the eye searches in vain; the bird is gone.'

The Dove Descending

The early Christians appropriated the dove, the bird of love and sacrifice, and transformed it into a symbol of the love of God and of the Holy Spirit:

> In those days Jesus came from Nazareth of Galilee and was baptized by John in the Jordan. And just as he was coming up out of the water, he saw the heavens torn apart and the Spirit descending like a dove on him. And a voice came from heaven, 'You are my Son, the Beloved; with you I am well pleased.'
>
> Mark 1:9–11

Gradually the dove became a central icon of the Holy Spirit in religious paintings, in church carvings, and, later, in stained-glass windows. The dove appeared repeatedly in depictions of the Annunciation in its guise as the Holy Spirit, often shown as impregnating Mary by a ray of golden light. An early El Greco painting from the mid-sixteenth century had the dove descending in a mighty golden cascade. Giambattista Tiepolo, two centuries later, the quintessential master of the Italian rococo style, in his vigorous *A Vision of the Trinity Appearing to Pope St. Clement*, painted a single dove in the foreground as it surfed on the leading edge of foaming billows of clouds bearing on them God the Father and God the Son.

Elsewhere the dove hovers over the head of Mary at the time of the birth of Jesus. A popular, if unorthodox, belief in the Middle Ages was that the conception must have taken place through Mary's ear – she heard the Word and in her it became flesh. A sixteenth-century German carving shows a dove alighting on the head of Mary, but with a halo over its head, not hers – possibly a doctrinal statement of the Reformation.

In the fourth century St. Gregory of Nyssa wrote, 'As the soul becomes enlightened . . . it takes the beautiful shape of a dove.' By this he implied that the Spirit grows within a person until the soul takes a godlike form. It is possible that St. Gregory was aware of the legend that at the martyrdom, in about 155 CE, of St. Polycarp, the elderly bishop of Smyrna, a dove was seen to leave his body as it was burned. When ordered to execrate Jesus Christ, the saint had answered, 'For 86 years I have been his servant and he has never done me wrong; how can I blaspheme my king who has saved me?'

The Gospel of the Dove

The dove has two wings, even as the Christian has two ways of life, the active and the contemplative. The blue feathers of the wings are thoughts of heaven; the uncertain shades of the body, the changing colors that recall an unquiet sea, symbolize the ocean of human passion in which the Church is sailing. Why are the dove's eyes this beautiful golden color? Because yellow, the color of ripe fruit, is the color too of experience and maturity, and the yellow eyes of the dove are the looks full of wisdom which the Church casts on the future. The dove, moreover, has red feet, for the Church moves through the world with her feet in the blood of martyrs.

> *De Bestris et Allis Rebus* by Hugh of Saint Victor (1096–1141)

The author of this 'gospel' was the medieval mystic and theologian known as Hugh of Saint Victor. Every creature, according to Hugh, could be 'read' as a sensible expression of divine thought.

The Dove Beloved

In the Song of Solomon, the passionate love poem of the Jewish Bible, the call of the Turtle Dove (*Stretopelia turtur*), and called here a 'turtle,' is seen as the harbinger of spring:

> My beloved spake, and said unto me,
> Rise up, my love, my fair one, and come away.
> For, lo, the winter is past,
> The rain is over and gone;
> The flowers appear on the earth;
> The time of the singing of birds is come,
> And the voice of the turtle is heard in our land.

> The Song of Solomon 2:10–12

Lewis and Clark found that the Native American tribes among whom they traveled in 1804 held the same belief: 'The dove is cooing, which is the signal, as the Indians inform us, of the approach of the salmon.' Similarly, George Caitlin, the nineteenth-century artist who spent many years among the Prairie Indians, recorded that the dove was seen by them as the messenger of the cycle of rebirth, which came to them not with the Mediterranean olive, but bearing willow leaves in its beak at the advent of spring. Chinese prognostications were more precise and personal: they believed the dove sang immediately after the vernal equinox (about March 20) and that, once heard, it brought the hearer good luck.

The bird's name in the Song of Solomon has nothing whatever to do with the relative of the tortoise. The Romans had a particular affection for the little dove with a plaintive cry; they called it *turtur* in imitation of its song. The French name for it – *tourterelle* – sounds even more like its sleepy, seductive call.

But it is the beauty of the dove that the poet recalls with great fervor again and again as a reflection of the beauty of the beloved:

> Ah, you are beautiful, my love;
> Ah, you are beautiful;
> Your eyes are doves.
>
> The Song of Solomon 1:15

Through the ages, the dove has embodied beauty, hope, gentleness, peace, and love in the world, heavenly attributes for which she became the symbol of God's presence in the world seen through this little creature. It is little wonder that Jesus sent his disciples out with the admonition that they must be 'as innocent as doves.'

Let an anonymous medieval poet have the last word.

The Nature of the Turtle Dove

> In a book the life of the turtle dove
> Is written in rhyme, how faithfully
> She keepeth her love throughout her life time.
> If once she should have a mate,
> From him she will not go.
> Women think about her life:
> I will tell it to you.
> By her mate she sits a-night,
> A-day they goeth and flyeth;
> Whoso says that they are sundered,
> I say that he lieth,

But if this mate of hers were dead,
And she widow were, Then flyeth she alone and fareth;
None other will she more,
But alone goeth and alone sits
And for her old love ever waits,
In her heart holding him night and day,
As if he were alive ay.

Meaning:

Listen, faithful men, hereto
And hereof often think:
Our soul when at the church's door,
Chooses Christ for her mate.
He alone is our soul's spouse,
Love we him with might,
And turn we never away from him,
By day or by night.
Though he be from our vision gone,
Be we to him all true,
No other Lord should we espouse,
Nor any lover new.
Believe we that he liveth ever,
Up in heaven's kingdom,
And he from there shall come again
And be to us all useful,
And for to judge the souls of men,
Not all of them the same:
His hated foes to hell shall fare,
His lovers to his realm.

4

The Eagle

Bless the Lord, O my Soul, and do not forget all his benefits . . . who satisfies you with good as long as you live so that your youth is renewed like the eagle's.

Psalm 103:2, 5

> He clasps the crag with crooked hands,
> Close to the sun in lonely lands,
> Ring'd with the azure world, he stands.
>
> The wrinkled sea beneath him crawls,
> He watches from the mountain walls,
> And like a thunderbolt he falls.

Alfred Lord Tennyson (1809–92)

Remote and inaccessible, the eagle seems to exist in ferocious disdain of lesser beings into whose lives it descends only as they become its victims. Swift and powerful killers, birds of prey use their keen eyesight to search out their quarry, strike it dead with their vicious talons, and then use their strong, curved beaks to rip it to pieces. The largest and fiercest of these winged predators, or raptors, is the eagle.

Eagles belong to the order Falconiformes, day-flying birds of prey, an order that also includes hawks, falcons, and vultures. There are at least 67 different types of eagle, and it is estimated that as a species it came into existence some 40 million years ago. In size, eagles range from one no bigger than a hawk to the huge Harpy Eagle of Central and South America, which has legs as thick as a child's wrist, a 9-inch toe span, and talons 1½ inches long. The Aztecs called it 'the winged wolf' because it will attack and kill animals much larger than itself. The African Crowned Eagle is known to regularly kill bushbuck weighing as much as 44 lbs., and the Golden Eagle, itself weighing only some 8 to 10 lbs., can carry a load of up to 15 lbs. weight. It was once authentically reported, from Sweden, that a Golden Eagle killed a mature roebuck of 66 lbs. With its vast territory (some 12,000 acres), the sheer savage majesty of its mien and form, its mountain habitat, high-soaring flight and prodigious killing skills, it is little wonder that the eagle holds the highest place in human imagination.

The Spiritual Eagle

'When thou seest an eagle,' wrote William Blake, 'thou seest a portion of genius.' From the dawn of civilization, this bird has been regarded as the epitome of power and authority, from the eagle gods of Babylon down through classical times to the national emblems of our own day. Since the Garuda, that great eagle of the Hindu pantheon (the sacred mount of Vishnu, 'the preserver'), warred against Naga, the earth serpent, in a deadly but ultimately triumphant conflict, the eagle has represented the heavenly and spiritual power contesting with the forces of darkness and of the earth. Shelley understood this: 'When Snake and Eagle meet – the world's foundations tremble,' he wrote in *The Revolt of Islam*. The Giant Eagle, the Rukh, springs from this myth and entered Indian fables dating back to the fourth century BCE, and is itself the prototype of the Roc of the later *Arabian Nights* stories featuring Sinbad the Sailor. Once, marooned on a desert island, Sinbad comes across an enormous white shiny dome-shaped object, which he mistakes for a building. It turns out to be the egg of the gigantic Roc, a bird so large it feeds its young on elephants. The monster returns, darkening the sky and raising a great wind with its wings and, as it settles on its egg, the ever-resourceful Sinbad ties himself to its leg, so hitching a lift when it flies off. Later, when he has freed himself, he sees the Roc snatch up a huge snake from the Valley of Diamonds and carry it thrashing about into the sky. So here is a recasting of the same power struggle.

In ancient Greek myths, the eagle is not only the symbol of the ascendance of spirit over matter, but becomes the instrument of justice, too. As the servant of Zeus, sovereign over all the gods, he fetches and carries the thunderbolts hurled by the god at his enemies. The eagle was also the enforcer of judgement in the story of Prometheus, the demigod who first created man, then – to relieve man's life of its suffering – stole fire from heaven. For this presumption, Zeus had him chained to a rock and condemned him to the everlasting torment of having his liver continuously pecked at by an eagle.

In the story of Ganymede, the surpassingly beautiful son of the king of Troy, the eagle has a different role. Zeus sent the eagle (or, in some versions of the story, disguised himself as one) to carry off the boy to be his cupbearer. The best understanding of the story is that Beauty (Ganymede) is given a place on Mount Olympus, the abode of the gods, as one of humankind's greatest blessings. Naturally, with its theme of Beauty inhabiting our highest achievements, the story inspired many artists, especially during the Renaissance, to recreate it in paint and sculpture, even to use it as a type or foretaste of

Christ's ascension to heaven. But Rembrandt, as so often, reflected on its emotional implications and painted Ganymede as a terrified child struggling in the clutches of a great alien bird (perhaps to mirror his own struggles as an artist against ill health, loss, and bankruptcy).

Curiously, and perhaps because of the bird's remote life, the eagle is largely absent from legends in northern Europe and appears only fleetingly in Celtic tales. But among the indigenous peoples of North America, it takes pride of place as the symbol of the Sun and Sky god, and concomitantly as the Thunderbird of lightning and storms. The American Indian icon for the eagle is often a cross, the pattern of its head, wings, and tail against the sky. Images of eagles and their feathers are used in many tribal arts, dances, and ceremonies. Pueblo Indians of the Southwest perform the Eagle Dance, and the ceremonial headdress of the Sioux has eagle feathers.

The Imperial Eagle

The eagle was sacred to Jupiter in Rome. At the funeral pyre of the god-king Augustus, it was said that an eagle had risen from the flames and taken his soul to heaven. So ever after, when a Roman emperor died, a live eagle was released into the sky to bear his soul on high.

It took just a small step to subvert the power of the eagle, once heavenly, to that which was earthly and political; for the eagle became the symbol of military might, of victory and leadership. Romans looked back to the day that Alexander the Great was born, and claimed the two eagles seen to perch on the roof of his birthplace were a sign of his future military prowess. The eagle became preeminent, Pliny tells us, in the second consulship of Marius (104 BCE), when he selected it for the figure on the standard for all Rome's legions. Since when, made of gilt or bronze with wings outstretched, it was borne aloft on its long pole into every battle (*aquilifer*, the Latin word for standard bearer, actually means 'eagle carrier'). An interesting descendant of the imperial eagle is found on the gold ampulla (a vessel holding anointing oils) used in the British coronation ceremony. On the vessel's lid is an eagle with spread wings.

A Roman eagle of particular notoriety was that set up by King Herod over the great gate of the Temple in Jerusalem. Some young men took it to be an insult to their faith, which forbade in the Ten Commandments the making of 'any graven image, or any likeness of anything that is in heaven above, or that is in the earth beneath.' When Herod was on his deathbed, the youths proceeded to pull down the offending eagle, and were consequently horribly punished by being burnt alive. This resulted in a public demonstration in sympathy for the young victims in response to which Achelaus, who had succeeded his father to the throne, ordered his army into the city and massacred a further 3,000 of the inhabitants in reprisal.

The eagle's checkered history continues with Charlemagne, who after his coronation in Rome in 800 CE adopted the eagle for his shield; and centuries later, Napoleon, vainglorious in his imitation of the Roman emperors, took the black eagle as his symbol. It later appeared notoriously on standards in the massed ranks of the Nazis at propaganda rallies in 1930s Germany.

But the eagle had become before that time a national emblem in Albania, Austria, Mexico, Poland, and many other countries, demonstrating humankind's faith in the lasting effectiveness of its symbolism. The two-headed eagle is the ultimate sign of imperial supreme power and was so used by the Hapsburg and Russian empires to demonstrate this. The 'double-tête' eagle has an ancient provenance stretching back to Hittite times, revived by the Seljuk Turks in the Middle Ages, and then taken up by the Crusaders into a European setting.

The Eagle and the Church

In Palestine, at least eight different kinds of eagle and vulture have been observed, but only one Hebrew word, *nesher*, was used to describe them all.

There are more than 30 references to the eagle in the Bible. Often it is the eagle's great speed of flight that captures the writer's imagination and is used to articulate what is admirable in humans, as when David laments the deaths of King Saul and his son Jonathan in battle on the mountains of Gilboa, and describes them as 'swifter than eagles, they were stronger than lions.' Another impressive use of the image is that by the prophet Obadiah to express man's vaunting ambition: 'Though thou exalt thyself as an eagle, and though thou set thy nest among the stars.' In the famous lines of Isaiah 40, the poet uses the flight of the eagle to reveal a wholly unexpected insight: 'But those who hope in the Lord will renew their strength. They will soar on wings like eagles,' reveling in the power of God to uplift the faithful.

In cathedrals and churches the reading desk that holds the Bible is frequently in the form of an eagle with outspread wings. Because of their ability to ascend high into the sky, the eagle lectern symbolizes both the 'high' inspiration of the Bible and the spreading of the Christian gospel all round the world. The symbol of St. John the Evangelist is an eagle, and of the four gospels, that of St. John has often been considered to have been written on the highest level of inspiration. St. John is often referred to as 'the winged eagle'; in Christian art he has been pictured as flying on the back of an eagle, his gaze piercing further into the mysteries of heaven than anyone else.

The Eagle Eye

To be eagle-eyed is to have keen or piercing eyesight, and part of eagle legend is that it can stare directly into the sun without being blinded. 'Nay, if thou be that princely eagle's bird, Show thy descent by gazing 'gainst the sun,' wrote Shakespeare (*Henry VI, Part III*). John Milton (1608–74) also referred to the eagle 'kindling her undazzled eyes at the full midday sun' (*Areopagitica*). Eagles were also believed to fly close to the sun as they grew older, to burn away the encroaching mist that was beginning to cloud their eyes. When they came back to earth they plunged three times into spring or sea water and so miraculously regained their youth and sprouted a fresh crop of feathers. These tales were probably an attempt to explain natural but mystifying behavior. With their huge wings, eagles are adept at using the thermal currents, like a glider, to lift them high into the sky and take them vast distances with a minimum of effort. To the observer on the ground, the bird must have seemed to all but disappear into the sun.

The mist before their eyes was probably the nictitating membrane – a bird's 'third eyelid.' The membrane is drawn across the eye to both clean and protect it, and only remains there when the bird is asleep. As for the renewal of youth story, it may well be a romantic telling of the bird's annual molt, which surely sounds better in the words of Edmund Spenser than as bald fact:

> An eagle fresh out of the ocean wave
> Where he left his plumes all hoary grey,
> And decks himself with feathers, youthful gay . . .
>
> Edmund Spenser (ca. 1552–99)

But the natural explanations contain also the spiritual dimension as taught in the medieval bestiaries. Christian preachers compared the eagle's unblinking flight into the blazing sun to Jesus Christ gazing on the dazzling glory of God before coming down to earth to save the soul of man. The mystical poet Angelus Silesius (1624–77), reflecting on Jesus Christ, adds the essentially human part of the relationship, 'Fearlessly the eagle looks the sun in the face, as you can stare at eternal brightness if your heart is pure.'

The eagle's renewal of life by plunging into the water was like Christian baptism, whereby we gain entry into the new life of salvation. Christians were told to 'break off all forms of worldliness on the rock of salvation,' just as the eagle 'breaks off the excessive growth of its beak in old age by hitting it against a rock.' Aristotle helped to spread the myth that in old age the upper part of the eagle's beak grew gradually longer and more crooked until the bird died of starvation. He appears to have muddled his facts, perhaps thinking of rodents' teeth which must be constantly ground down by gnawing.

One story queries the eagle's legendary eyesight. Aeschylus, the Greek poet, had been warned that he would meet his death from a weight falling on his bald head. So he stayed out in the open. But an eagle at a great height, mistaking his bald head for a rock, dropped a tortoise on it, in order to break open the creature's shell. Aeschylus died. 'Certainly,' Sir Thomas Browne wrote, 'it was a very great mistake in the perspicacity of that animal.'

The Eagle Inn Sign

Eagles were and are widely used on inn signs in Britain. The Eagle and Child (sometimes 'The Bird and Baby') is one of the more unusual ones. It is the crest of the Stanley family, the earls of Derby, and has a curious story attached to its origins. In the fourteenth century in the reign of Edward III, it is said that the wife of one of the Stanleys gave birth to an illegitimate son and pretended that she had found the child in an eagle's nest and adopted him. (It was suspected that eagles could snatch a baby from its cradle, but it always remained unproven.) The story obviously stuck in this instance.

Another inn features in a popular nineteenth-century song,

now sung by children as a nursery rhyme, which has the lines:
'Up and down the City Road,/In and out the Eagle,/That's
the way the money goes/Pop goes the weasel.' This refers to a
spendthrift drinker going into his East End pub in London,
the Eagle in the City Road, and having to pawn (pop) his be-
longings to get back some money with which to feed himself.

The Eagle: Hunted or Hunter

Humans have plundered eagles since time immemorial. When
Aeschylus wanted to describe, in his tragedy *Agamemnon* in
the fifth century BCE, the grief of heroes as they set off for the
Trojan War, he wrote:

> Then loud their warlike anger cried
> As eagles cry, that wild with grief
> Above their robbed nest wheel and sail . . .

In eighteenth-century Britain, eagles were classed as vermin
and churchwardens gave the substantial sum of 12 pence for
each carcass. In a later period, their nests were raided for eggs
(a task made easier by the nests' great size and annually re-
used site) to requite the Victorians' collection mania, for skins
gathered for the taxidermist's skills, and they were also
slaughtered in the interests of game preservation. This attitude continued unabated until the bird had been banished, as
is the case today, to the remoter parts of Scotland and
Northern Ireland. We can remember with regret that Welsh
poets once called Snowdon 'Caer Eryi,' the camp of eagles.

In 1784 an eagle in the Museum of Natural History in Paris
went completely off its food and began to mope. It was
offered a live cock to eat in the hope that this would stimulate
its appetite and save its life. However, as soon as the birds
were put together, the eagle, so it is said, put a protective wing
over the smaller bird and they 'strolled about together.' The

eagle fully recovered its health – perhaps it had just been suffering from loneliness. Shakespeare hinted that eagles have a gentler side – 'the eagle does suffer little birds to sing.'

The Golden Eagle is the only eagle known to have been trained by man to hunt. As early as 2000 BCE, eagles 'flew to the fist' in China, where the Tartars used them to catch antelopes. However, this eagle seizes its prey on the ground, so its popularity would have been limited among the 'hawking' fraternity, who prefer to launch their charges at airborne prey.

The American Bald Eagle

It was in 1782 that the Bald Eagle was selected as a national symbol of the United States by the Continental Congress. But not without controversy, for Benjamin Franklin among others was privately unhappy with the choice. He wrote to his daughter that the eagle was unworthy to represent 'the brave and honest Republic of America,' describing it as 'a rank coward, a bird of bad moral character that lived by sharping [cheating] and robbing.' (The bird does eat carrion and poaches fish from the osprey in particular.) Franklin preferred the Wild Turkey, 'a much more respectable bird, and withal a true original of America . . . a bird of courage, and would not hesitate to attack a grenadier of the British Guards, who should presume to invade his farmyard with a red coat on.' Despite opposition the eagle was chosen, and in 1787 became the official emblem of the United States of America. Though the story may be apocryphal, it was said that witnesses at early battles of the Revolution reported that eagles were seen circling above 'shrieking for Freedom,' and this explained Congress's choice. Their presence may have had more sinister purposes: as early as 937 CE an Anglo-Saxon saga of the battle of Brunanburh describes birds of prey swooping down to feast on the corpses on the battlefield: '. . . food for the grey feathered, white-tailed eagle, carrion to glut the greedy war hawk. . . . '

John Audubon was so impressed by his first sighting of the eagle in 1814 on the upper Mississippi River that he wanted to call it 'the Washington Eagle.' 'It is indisputably the noblest bird of its genus that has yet been discovered in the United States,' he claimed. A sighting of the eagle was equally inspiring to the future inventor Solomon Andrews. As a small boy daydreaming out of the window of his father's Presbyterian church in Perth Amboy, New Jersey, he spied an eagle gliding effortlessly in the blue skies. Its flight so fired his imagination that almost half a century later, in 1863, he invented the self-propelled, steerable airship.

But Franklin's turkey was far from ignored. It played a central role in the first Thanksgiving celebrations of the Pilgrims and remained a staple of the colonial diet. William Byrd II on his epic commission in 1728 to define the boundary – the 'dividing line' – between Virginia and North Carolina adopted the turkey's 'beard' as his commission's badge. Their very survival had depended on shooting the bird for food during their long and arduous journey in the wilderness. In the bird's honor, he created a mock 'Order of the Turkey Beard' with a 'beard' in their hats as a 'Cocquade' and the motto *Vice Cotumicum* ('instead of quails') – the quails that had sustained Moses and the children of Israel on their long wanderings in the wilderness!

The Bald Eagle, as its scientific name *Haliaeetus leucocephalus* implies – *halo* is 'sea,' *aeetos* is 'eagle,' *leukos* is 'white,' and *cephalos* is 'head' – is actually white-headed (rather than bald like a vulture) and inhabits the sea coastline. It is part of the family Accipitridae, together with hawks and kites, and when the first Europeans arrived in North America the Bald Eagle's population was some 100,000 nesting pairs. By 1963 only 417 known nesting pairs were still in existence in the 48 continental states, the majority killed off by habitat loss, pesticides, and lead poisoning. Today the number of nesting pairs has climbed back to 7,000 to 8,000 due to strong endangered species and environmental protection laws, as well as many public and private conservation efforts. In addition, tens of thousands of Bald Eagles live in Alaska and Canada.

5

The Falcon

If the eagle is the real king of birds, then the falcon is the prince, his lithe fluent elegance a foil to the other's august, proud presence. Whether in flight or at rest, the two of them stand apart from other birds by the special grace and beauty they bring to the skies and by the sheer ferocity of their hunting prowess. Humankind has always admired this combination, and from early times has attempted to harness their killing skills both for the hunt, and to furnish the banqueting board.

What's in a Name?

Originally, 'hawk' and 'falcon' were used interchangeably for birds of prey, and still today both are called raptors (those who seize their victims), and likewise both belong to the order Falconiformes. 'Hawk' has a more ancient lineage, the name derived from the Old English word *hafoc*, with a strong association with the word 'havoc,' meaning 'destruction.' 'Cry havoc and let loose the dogs of war,' Shakespeare wrote in *Henry V*, an apt summary of the bird's lifestyle. We use the term 'hawk' to describe an aggressive person, as opposed to a peace-loving 'dove.' And it is also used for a stern opponent, as in Hawkeye, the hero of James Fenimore Cooper's 'Leatherstocking' novel *The Last of the Mohicans*.

The word 'falcon' was only introduced, at least in literary form, to the English language in 1250, from the French *faucon*, a 'sickle or reaping hook,' accurately describing the shape and power of the bird's beak and talons. Also in the order Falconiformes are the kite, osprey, harrier, and the eagle, too – birds of prey that hunt by day, as opposed to the order Strigiformes – owls – who hunt by night.

However, there is much to distinguish between falcons and hawks. The latter's territory consists of woodland and brush, their shortish, broad wings necessary aids among stands of trees, allowing them swift changes in direction and great maneuverability from their long tails. Their Latin name of *accipiter*, 'swift-flying,' acknowledges this quick, and secretive, flight pattern, particularly as seen in their sudden attacks from a concealed perch on small birds.

Three species of the true hawk (the genus *Accipiter*) occur in North America: the Sharp-shinned Hawk ('Sharpie'), the Cooper's Hawk (the 'chicken hawk' of colonial America), and the Northern Goshawk, the largest of the three. Hawks have sharply hooked bills, powerful feet with hooked, sharp claws (talons), and excellent vision, several times more accurate than humans with good eyesight. They all start out with yellow eyes as juveniles, which later change to orange, then red.

'Hawk' is often used loosely as the common name of birds in various parts of the world. In North America, for example, members of the genus *Buteo* are called 'hawks,' while they are known as buzzards in Europe.

Falcons, a world-wide genus of 38 species, have blunt heads, slim bodies, and long, narrow, pointed wings. They are distinguished from others in their order as they do not build nests and they have two teeth on the mandible for breaking the necks of their prey before feeding on it. They also hunt from a great height, a feature not exclusive to them, but unlike hawks.

The Peregrine (*Falco peregrinus*) holds pride of place among falcons on account of its sheer power, precision, and speed. It is also cosmopolitan and will travel ('peregrinate') wherever is necessary for survival, from sea level to mountain-top, from desert to tropical forest. When hunting, falcons have been known to rise to 15,000 feet, then pinpoint their victims with their especially adapted eyesight, before diving, or 'stooping,' at devastating speed with closed wings. A pere-grine's vertical dive has been timed in excess of 180 mph. It has to have special baffles in its nostrils so that it can continue to breathe and that the in-rushing air does not burst its lungs. The force of the impact is often so severe that the victim's head can be broken off entirely.

The male peregrine is known as the *tiercel* because it is one third (from the Old French *tierce*) smaller than the female (1 lb. 3 oz. compared to 1 lb. 14 oz.). This gender disparity is found in other birds of prey, suggesting nature's precautionary measure to safeguard the female during mating from the feroc-ity of the male. But the term *gentil* or 'gentle' is applied to the female bird, in the sense of noble, a 'gentlewoman,' no less!

Falcons of Old

In early millennia, the sight of falcons flying high in the intense light of the sun captured the spiritual imagination of humans. In Egypt, the bird became the embodiment of the heavenly spaces and of light in the form of Horus ('the lofty one'), the falcon-headed, a dynamic aspect of the sun god and chief of gods, Ra. The whole sky was imagined as a falcon traveling the firmament on speckled wings, opening his eyes alternately, the right (beneficent) eye the sun, and the left (sinister) the moon. The bird's link to the sun is seen in many statues of Horus, where his head is framed in a half disc radi-ating beams of light. And his dark side is revealed by Horus's constant companion, Uraeus, the poisonous asp of death. Jewelers fashioned necklaces and pectorals incorporating the falcon in gold, turquoise, and lapis to protect their wearers from the forces of darkness. From the tomb of Tutankhamun came a magnificent example in which the bird holds in one talon the sign for life, and in the other the sign for eternity.

To avail themselves of the eternal life-giving properties of the falcon, Egyptians killed, mummified, then finally buried them in sarcophagi in underground galleries beside the dead – 800,000 falcons have been found in Saqqara in Lower Egypt alone. This is a small measure beside the 4 million sacred ibis also interred there! Ibis were the bird embodiment of Thoth, lord of creation, resurrection, and the arts of peace, all essential components of the afterlife.

An actual falcon was substituted for Horus at the coronation of a new pharaoh, a sign of immortality and enlightenment. So too at the court of the Peruvian Incas, but there it played the role of guardian angel and spiritual brother. These signs bring to mind the descent of the Spirit in the form of a dove at Jesus's baptism.

In the classical world, the falcon was not only the sun god Apollo's familiar, but became also a bird of oracle and good omen as befitted the companion of the god of prophecy and divination. In Homer's *Odyssey*, falcons nest by Calypso's cave, a good omen that the hero will eventually complete his journey. In the same epic, there is Circe, the enchantress, whose name means 'she-falcon' (*circ-circ* is the sound of the bird's cry). She, like the bird, can be pitiless, turning the hero's sailors into animals, but Odysseus's stay with her again augurs well for his homecoming.

Mortal warriors, too, adopted the bird of prey as their living symbol: Attila the Hun chose a hawk as his emblem, although not necessarily the falcon. Its fearlessness, its supreme killing skills, and its fierce and noble mien were all part of its attraction to men who prided themselves on having like qualities.

The Noble Art

One day he saw a galaxy of ladies ride by . . .
Each had a falcon on her wrist,
And to the river in the plain
They passed. The prey rose up amain,
Cormorants, herons, mallards flew;
The falcons soared with proud disdain,
Stooped, and each hawk his quarry slew.

Sir Orfeo (mid-fourteenth century)

Human admiration for raptors led to a desire to tame them, leading to the most ancient practice and sport of falconry. It can be traced back to 2000 BCE at least, to Egypt, where it is vividly illustrated in wall paintings from the tombs of the Pharaohs. From there it spread to Arabia, India, China, and Japan, and eventually to Europe.

What had been once a common pursuit became, in time, a royal prerogative, fit only for kings and the aristocrats of their courts. A magnificent illustration of the 'sport of kings' from chariots, as it spread throughout the Middle East, is sculpted in the Assyrian bas-reliefs at Khorsabad in Iraq, dating from the ninth century BCE. Later, in Persian miniature paintings, and through epic stories and poems, we find how the Mogul emperor Shah Jahan and Kublai Khan, the grandson of Genghis Khan, invested the sport with an oriental magnificence. Thomas Bewick mentions the Chinese love of hawking; their peculiar speciality was the training of small hawks to catch butterflies.

Falconry reached Europe in 300 BCE and came via France to Britain, where both the Saxon King Ethelbert (860–65 CE) and King Alfred the Great were alleged to own falcons. Ownership of prized birds of chase became widespread and zealously guarded: Henry II sent for falcons to Pembrokeshire in 1173; some 40 years later King John was seeking them in County

Antrim in Ireland. The Bayeux Tapestry shows King Harold with a hawk on his fist. And when Edward III invaded France in the mid-fourteenth century, the chronicler Froissart records that he took with him 30 falconers on horseback. Robert of Avenel (in the twelfth century) made just one stipulation as he granted his lands in Dumfriesshire to the Abbey of Melrose: he reserved the rights to all falcon-nesting sites.

In the fifteenth century the bishop of St. Albans was appointed to the title of Grand Falconer, a position of great prestige as shown by the post's annual stipend of £1,000. Five hundred years later, one of the guests invited to the coronation of Queen Elizabeth II in 1953 was the duke of St. Albans, who still retained the hereditary title. In his acceptance, the twelfth duke announced that he was going to bring along to Westminster Abbey for the ceremony a live falcon. Permission for this was withheld, but a stuffed bird was allowed. The Grand Falconer objected to the injunction and declined the invitation altogether.

The person who trains and flies falcons is called, naturally, a 'falconer,' but the man of hawks is not a 'hawker,' but an 'austringer' from the Old French for a Goshawk.

Pecking Order

Crusaders returning from the Near East in the Middle Ages gave a new impetus to falconry. But the rigid feudal class system decided to define and classify its pastime. Dame Juliana Barnes's *Boke of St Albans*, printed in 1486, carried a detailed list of the hierarchy of hunting birds and their permitted owners. Thus, only kings could carry the rare, migratory Gyrfalcon, while the Peregrine was preserved for princes, earls and dukes, and the Sparrow Hawk ('a small ignoble bird') was the lot of priests. The 'Lady's Hawk' – still so named today – was the diminutive Merlin, weighing some four to five ounces, and in size not much bigger than a blackbird, the French *merle*, which gives it its name; it was just right for the wrist of a lady. Merlins were lark hunters, chasing the songster in ascending spirals until the lark would drop back to earth at great speed to seek cover and elude capture. Larks (particularly larks' tongues) were then much valued as table delicacies, so again the Merlin was a suitable hawk for a lady. Yeomen were only allowed the Goshawk, a contraction of goose-hawk. It was also known as *cuisinier* or 'cook's bird,' so-called for its ability to stock the larder not only with geese, but its other staple quarry of pigeons and rabbits, essentials for the medieval table.

To the least of servants was left the Kestrel, an unbiddable bird for the falconer's skills. So the name became synonymous with a worthless fellow, as plainly stated in these lines from Spenser's *Faerie Queene*:

> No thought of honour ever did assay
> His baser brest; but in his kestrel kind
> A pleasant veine of glory he did find
>
> Edmund Spenser (ca. 1552–99)

Likewise, the buzzard was given a low rating, being called a coward and slothful to boot – a reputation no doubt based on its love of carrion, or its habit of slowly wheeling round the sky to no apparent purpose.

The Hobby Falcon (*Falco subbuteo*) may derive its name from the French *hoberau*, an impoverished noble or a small squire, which would explain its lowly place in Dame Juliana's listing. Dragonflies and other insects form its diet outside the breeding season, another cause for complaint. However, it is probably more likely to come from the German *hober*, 'to stir,' arising from how it attacks a flock of starlings, by swooping among them suddenly and, in the 'stirring up' confusion, selects one for the kill. Incidentally, Cervantes's Don Quixote called it a 'Robin Ruddock' on account of its plumage color.

As with this strict order of human ownership, so with the

natural order: any transgression of nature's laws was an omen of impending doom and chaos. In Shakespeare's *Macbeth*, an old man with ironic innocence foretells the murder of good King Duncan:

> On Tuesday last
> A falcon, towering in her pride of place
> Was by a mousing owl hawked at, and killed.

Coming to Terms

The rich and vibrant intercourse of birds and humans led to an enrichment of the English language with a whole range of falconry terms. Many of these are still current today, although meanings may have altered or indeed changed altogether.

The word 'bate' meant 'to fly from the fist after quarry' or to 'fly off the fist in fear,' both involving a great fluttering of wings. Nowadays when you say someone is 'in a bate,' you are saying he is angry: you could say, in fact, that the wing movements have become flying fists or whirling arms.

When two or several birds were set at a large quarry such as a heron, it was called 'a cast of hawks'; 'cast' was also used to describe the process when a bird vomits up, or 'hawks up,' a pellet of indigestible skin, bones, and feather from its stomach, while a 'casting' was its excrement; the word also meant 'to set a bird off from the fist.' Today it is still used to mean excrement as in 'worm casts,' and is used for the 'casting' of molten material into molds to make such objects as bells. But by casting we also mean 'throwing': you 'cast off' a boat from its mooring because you throw the rope on board; 'Ne'er cast a clout 'til May is out' may be an old country aphorism, but it is still commonly heard. Another sense is also found in the 'casting' of a theatrical play, meaning to throw it open to actors to contest for the best parts. A common slang expression meaning to drink alcoholic drink is 'to booze,' and where you do it is 'the boozer.' 'Bowse' was the falconry term for bringing a bird to a drinking place.

When a hawking party set out, it was usual to take more birds than could be carried on each person's fist. To do this you had a 'cadge,' a portable perch, on which several falcons could be carried at any one time. It fitted on to a 'cadger's' shoulders, like a backpack, allowing him free movement of his hands on foot or on horseback. Our present-day term, 'cadger,' meaning one who asks for money or favors, probably originates in the ability of the perch carrier to tell tall stories to gullible passersby about the birds on his back and so to solicit money from them for the privilege.

'Lure' has an interesting history: it signified the bird, in particular a pigeon, traditionally used to catch an adult hawk. The method was to tether the victim to a post by a piece of string long enough to allow it to move about and attract the hawk's attention, but not for it to escape. The bird was literally a 'stool pigeon,' a person the police use as a decoy or an informant.

In the nineteenth century the unfortunate bird, while being used to entrap its fellow Passenger Pigeons, had its eyelids sewn together to prevent it giving the game away. It was also the name for the feathered decoy to which were attached small pieces of meat with which falconers taught their birds to fly back to the fist. To 'lure' someone has come to mean to tempt or attract by means of an award.

During the molting season birds were at risk and so confined to a building known as the 'mews' (from the French *muer*, meaning 'to molt'). For 160 years, between 1377 and 1537, the royal mews were at Charing Cross in London. Then Henry VIII decided to house his horses on the site and the word took on the new meaning of 'stables' for horses. With the decline in horse transport, property developers saw their potential, and these stables were turned into bijou town dwellings or pieds-à-terre, complete with garage, where the horse or carriage once sheltered, and the name 'mews house' was coined. 'To mew' is to cry like a hawk, but also, by happenstance, like a kitten or cat.

Trappings and Suits

The equipment used in falconry has changed little over the years. A thick leather 'gauntlet,' or glove, covers usually the left hand, to protect it from the vice-like grip of the bird's talons as it perches. Soft leather strips, 'jesses,' are attached to the bird's legs at one end, and at the other to the top ring of a swivel. Through the other ring is looped a leash with which to tether the bird. At times a leather hood is placed over the head to serve as a temporary blindfold – 'to hoodwink' the bird. The hood was traditionally decorated with feathers – the most favored were those of the heron.

This large water bird provided rich sport for the nobility (as it did for Chaucer's franklin), for it needed the concerted attention of up to three trained birds to bring it down. An old name for a heron was a 'hearnshaw,' and the saying 'to know a hawk from a handsaw' (as found in Shakespeare's *Hamlet*) is a corruption of the word and means to be able to distinguish one thing from another, such as a predator from its prey.

The hooded falcon became a byword for that hope in the light which is nourished in darkness. Renaissance printers adopted it as their emblem with the verbal device *Post Tenebras Spero Lucem* – 'After darkness I hope for light.'

Training Manual

A book written in 1248 by Emperor Frederick II of Hohenstaufen – *De Arte Venandi cum Avibus* (*The Art of Hunting with Birds*) – describes methods of catching, keeping, training, and flying birds of prey that are still standard practice today. You could either start with 'eyeasses,' nestlings that had to be taught to hunt from scratch, taking many weeks for what in the wild would have been achieved in a few days, or capture 'passage-hawks' as mature adults during migration, which only had to be tamed. This is probably the origin of the name 'peregrine.'

The training was arduous for man and bird. Birds of prey have no apparent instinct of fear, so cannot be subdued by threats. The proven method was for falconer and bird to spend days and nights beside each other until exhaustion, hunger, and familiarity enticed the bird on to the falconer's fist. It could take nine days at a stretch. The book called *The Goshawk* by T. H. White gives a marvelous insight into the method. In it he quotes a proverb, which helps our understanding of the profound relationship that develops between the trainer and his bird, Gos: 'When your first wife dies, she makes such a hole in your heart that all the rest slip through.'

That training a bird of prey generates intense feelings is also revealed in an anonymous German poem dated to 1160 and translated as follows, which can be understood literally or as a poem of human love:

> I trained myself a falcon for more than a year.
> And when I trained him and made him my dear
> And wound his feathers around with gold and silver strands
> He towered up and flew off to another's lands.

> I saw my falcon later flying high and fair
> With silken jesses on his feet he was not want to wear
> And his pretty plumage shining red with gold.
> May God bring them together whose love is still unfold.

Petruchio's speech about 'taming' Katherine in Shakespeare's *Taming of the Shrew* is full of falconry training terms, as familiar to the Tudor audience as the innuendos of many hues that it contains:

> My falcon now is sharp and passing empty
> And, 'till she stoop, she must not be full-gorged,
> For then she never looks upon her lure
> Another way I have to man my haggard,[1]
> To make her come, and know her keeper's call,
> That is to watch her, as we watch those kites
> That bate, and beat, and will not be obedient.
> She ate no meat today, nor none shall eat.
> Last night she slept not, nor tonight she shall not.

Knowledge of hawks, however acquired, was a 'must' for the Elizabethan parvenu, as was evident to Ben Jonson's Stephen, in *Every Man in his Humour*, when he asks his uncle Kno'well to lend him a book so he can read up on the subject:

> an a man have not skill in the hawking, and the hunting-languages nowadays, I'll not give a rush for him. They are more studied than the Greek and the Latin. He is for no gallants' company without 'em.

Plus ça change . . .

Weapons of Mass Destruction

The regard in which man held his bird of prey was such that he attempted to improve his ordnance by naming it after them. Into the language came *faucon*, *fauconnette*, *robinette*, and *saker*, to describe small-bore culverins, or cannons. 'Robinette' is linked to the hobby falcon since it is a diminutive of the name. And even when the invention of the hand-

---

[1] 'Haggard' is a wild female hawk captured in full adult plumage.

held gun began to displace falconry as a means of procuring game, the new weapon was called a 'musket,' the name of the male Sparrow Hawk.

But its invention initiated a new relationship between birds of prey and humans: one of competition rather than collaboration – to the detriment of both.

Muzzle-loaders gave way to the breech-loader, and with its mechanism for rapid fire a new era came into being. In the social round of the countryside, house-party hosts rivaled one another over 'bags' – the number of game birds slaughtered. The birds were often reared artificially and intensively for that purpose only. Bags in excess of 1,000 were not unusual; 3,000 betokened a 'good day.' Birds of prey were seen as a threat to this sport, and ruthless methods were employed to safeguard the gamekeepers' stocks.

Far worse, though, than a shrinking habitat or game-keeper's blood lust was the introduction of pesticides. These enter the food chain through small birds and mammals, so that when eaten by the birds of prey the toxins are powerful enough to result in malformation of the embryos, for them to be stillborn, or for eggs to be soft-shelled. Such eggs either do not develop, or are crushed underfoot in the nest, or are at far greater risk from egg thieves such as the crow.

In World War II, peregrine falcons in Britain were hunted down mercilessly by government order. They posed a threat to carrier pigeons bearing important messages, especially those of aircrew who had ditched off the south coast.

The hunter's insatiable craving for his sport has resulted in migrating birds being subjected to wanton killing as they follow well-worn and seasonal paths. As the birds cross from Europe into North Africa, it is estimated that many millions of protected species are killed in Italy alone, each year. A similar figure is attributed to Spain.

A more curious killing field is found in the deserts of Arab countries, where hunting from camel or horseback has been overtaken by that from Land Rovers. The sight of 100 vehicles abreast, falcons on the fist, is not uncommon, with the result that the birds' natural quarry has all but disappeared. This has led to forays into parts of Africa where conservation measures have become necessary.

People in Glass Houses . . .

Even after the introduction of the modern firearm, birds of prey could still provide the only solution to certain predicaments.

Shortly after the Crystal Palace was built in London, in 1851, to house the Great Exhibition, sparrows took advantage not only of the warmth and shelter, but of the several trees planted in its interior. Soon their droppings were fouling the pathways and exhibits, not to mention 'bombing' the spectators themselves. The use of guns was obviously impossible. Out of desperation Queen Victoria appealed to the duke of Wellington for advice. 'Try sparrow hawks, Ma'am,' was his terse reply. She did. It worked.

City Dwellers

The Kestrel's names in old dialect are *standgale* and *windhover*, which describe its astonishing skills in riding the wind. Their German name, *Turmfalke*, 'tower falcon,' long predates a remarkable recent development: from Berlin and Munich to London and New York, Kestrels have taken to city life, where they nest on high buildings as a substitute for natural cliffs. The Kestrel is the smallest falcon living in New York City's five boroughs, feeding on insects, mice, and sparrows. Peregrines, too, have made a comeback in urban centers like New York and Chicago in recent years, each with over a dozen falcon couples living on top of high-rise apartment buildings, church steeples, and bridges.

The Windhover

With its subtitle 'to Christ our Lord,' Gerard Manley Hopkins wrote a sonnet about the Kestrel. In it he expresses, with a rich intensity of emotion in language of matching depth and scope, the Kestrel's consummate mastery of flight, its fitness to its element of air, and its unsurpassable grace. In dramatic contrast are his own poor attempts, as a Jesuit priest, to follow his Lord. The language is loaded with stresses and alliteration, which highlight his strong feelings and connect each thought and image to its sequel. A complicated series of images merge in the last six lines: a knight of chivalry riding into battle, the fire of Pentecost, the red blood of martyrs and the embers of their stakes, with the golden crowns of the saints on the one hand, then the contrast of laboring through heavy plowed soil, or raking the embers of a fire in order to reveal the heart of flame or the furrows' gleaming promise. The most central theme, perhaps, is that of the falcon in his flight, this creature of the air in all its grace and beauty and control, challenging us to rise above our earthly station as, simultaneously, it demonstrates the divine grace of the Saviour gloriously stooping down to us on this earth:

I caught this morning's minion, king-
   dom of daylight's dauphin, dapple-dawn-drawn falcon, in his riding
   Of the rolling level underneath him steady air, and striding
High there, how he rung upon the rein of a wimpling wing
In his ecstasy! Then off, off forth on swing,
   As a skate's heel sweeps smooth on a bow-bend; the hurl and gliding
   Re-buffed the big wind. My heart in hiding
Stirred for a bird – the achieve of, the mastery of the thing!

Brute beauty and valour and act, oh air, pride, plume, here
    Buckle! AND the fire that breaks from thee then, a billion
Times lovelier, more dangerous, O my chevalier!

    No wonder of it; sheer plod makes plough down sillion
Shine, and blue-bleak embers, ah my dear,
    Fall, gall themselves, and gash gold-vermilion.

Gerard Manley Hopkins (1844–89)

Words for Noises

There are special words for the distinctive sounds of birds.
Here are some. Blackbirds, sandpipers, and thrushes *whistle*.
Bitterns *boom*. Ravens and rooks *caw*. Doves *coo*. Sparrows
chirp. Jays and magpies *chatter*. Swallows *titter*. Gulls
squawk. Geese and swans *hiss*. Nightingales *pipe* – originally
from the Latin *pipare*, to chirp. Hens *cackle*. Cocks *crow*.
Turkeys *gobble*. Ducks *quack*. Owls *hoot*. Crows *croak*.
Hawks, eagles, and peacocks *scream*. Falcons, however, *chant*.

6

The Goose

Humans and geese have been in a domestic relationship for at least 6,000 years. But long before that, evidence contained in bone fragments found in the cave middens (rubbish heaps) of Old Stone Age man (35,000–8000 BCE) shows that already the wild goose was a quarry within his hunting skills. But it was 600,000 years ago that the wild goose first flew into archaeological history, predating humans by hundreds of millennia. And from not long afterwards – in geological time terms – we even have an accurate identification of a present-day species, the Brant or Brent Goose, discovered in a cave complex in England's West Country.

So the goose will have been part of human consciousness from the very beginning. Was the bird most remembered from those high-flying skeins in arrowhead, wedge, or curved formation, perennially marking the season's change at autumn and spring? Or was it the massed white wing-beat descent as geese flocks cascaded from great heights onto their grazing grounds? Or perhaps the prime memory is an aural one, because of their unmistakable honking and yipping calls? For the

urban dweller of today, it may well be domestic geese which take pride of place on river, canal, and estuary, swimming in line ahead like well-drilled men o' war, the large gander in pole position, his wives in tow, and a string of goslings bobbing out behind. From its early appearance among the bones in the caves of our ancestors, through myth, legend, and folktale, in nursery rhyme and pantomime, the goose has been our familiar and companion. It is therefore wholly fitting that the United States should choose the wild goose on the wing as its emblem for the National Wildlife Refuge System – for its partial domestication has only served to accentuate the unbounded freedom the goose enjoys in its wild state.

The Goose of Its Kind

'Goose' in its origins is one of the oldest words of the Indo-European languages. In the family Anatidae (which also includes swans and ducks) there are basically two kinds of true goose: the Grey or genus *Anser*, and the Brown or Brant, the genus *Branta* (the old word means charred or burnt). All domestic geese are descended from the European Greylag (*Anser anser*), except for the Chinese Goose which has evolved from the Swan Goose (*Anser cygnoides*). (The 'Sea Goose,' the Merganser, although containing the word 'anser' in its name, is a saw-toothed bird half-duck and half-diver, but no goose.)

In the wild, these large birds with webbed feet appear almost as much at home in open waters as on land, since their legs, placed well forward, allow them to walk freely, if with a somewhat ungainly gait. Yet, with the exception of the Canada Goose (*Branta canadensis*), and the Greylag Goose, the birds breed on the faraway Arctic tundra, so we rarely see their nesting sites or their very young in our own environment. Geese also yearly molt their wing feathers, and retire for safety for long periods to the water. Their diet consists mostly of aquatic plants, grasses, and grains, with a smattering of insects, except for the Brant (*Branta bernicla*), which is primarily a sea goose and has a particular liking for molluscs and crustaceans. Geese are strong and determined flyers, reaching speeds in excess of 60 miles an hour sustained over long migration flights. Their flight patterns are aerodynamic – the familiar V-formation allows each bird to fly in the slipstream of the goose in front, thus reducing drag and increasing their overall speed. But careful observation has revealed that no one bird dominates or leads – all share the point position and all benefit equally. And the spirit of group endeavor is sustained even if a bird drops out of formation, for two others will follow the ailing bird and stay with it until it either dies or rejoins the others.

It is possible that geese were the first birds domesticated by humans, for their habits made capture easier than with most other species. Geese are meadow-grass (or seaweed, or eel-grass) grazers, and assemble in large flocks on inland and coastal waters; and their appearance is predictable, for they return annually to their feeding areas at set times of the year. Their folk and dialect names, Stubble goose or Lag or Lea (meadow) goose, Bean goose, Corn goose, and Ware (seaweed) goose show us how they were identified by the crops and fodder they shared with humans.

Geese are also hardy birds and easily reared, becoming firmly attached to the hand that feeds them. In 1930 Konrad Lorenz, the famous naturalist and Nobel Prize winner, observed how easily a goose becomes attached to a human person, and suggested they were the most suitable of all creatures, next to the dog, for human companionship. Recently, a French ultralight aircraft enthusiast has demonstrated this 'follow the leader' instinct by training his birds from birth to accompany him as he flies.

Despite folklore to the contrary, geese also have a reputation for intelligence, combined with strong family and flock bonding. Once paired, geese will publicly proclaim their new bond in an elaborate 'triumph-calling' ceremony that involves much stretching of their necks and greeting each other with loud honking calls. The pair then remain faithful to one another for life, and the bond extends to the wider family, so that if a partner is lost, the survivor will seek out its siblings or its own parents, seldom ever taking another partner.

In China, the remarkable constancy of geese family ties inspired the traditional custom of giving a pair of the birds to a newlywed couple as a symbol of lifelong fidelity.

A Goose Legend

One of the stories the Chumash Indians of the southern California coast tell is called 'The Boys who turned to Geese':

A long time ago when animals were people, there lived a little boy whose mother and stepfather rejected him. He was very unhappy and very hungry, too, as no one looked to his needs. Another little boy, who had also been rejected, joined up with him. Racoon, seeing their plight and feeling sorry for them, taught them how to dig for roots. Five more little boys soon asked to join them and Racoon, and they all went into the *temescal* [sweathouse] to discuss their sad state. Finally it was agreed they all should go to the Far North Land and take Racoon with them.

So they covered themselves all over with goose down and sang the songs of journeys. For three days round and round the *temescal* they went – all seven of them and Racoon. Then higher and higher they began to rise into the air. All that is, except Racoon, who simply couldn't get the hang of flying. Soon many of the people came in begging them to stop what they were doing and to come back to them. But it was too late. All the little boys had turned into wild geese, and off they flew to the Far North Land. And when they arrived there they were transformed once again, becoming the seven stars we now call the Pleiades.

So when the wild geese fly calling overhead, the Chumash Indians say these are the voices of little boys, unhappy little boys, flying unwanted to places far away.

Mythic Goose

In the Ennead (the Egyptian pantheon) Seb, the earth god and father of the gods, is often depicted with a goose sitting on his head, an ideogram of his name. Moreover, certain legends describe him as a gander (the male goose), 'The Great Cackler,' whose female day after day lays the egg from which the sun emerges. This symbolic importance of the goose has its best statement in the magnificent wall painting of the 'Geese of Meidum,' one of the most impressive artistic images of ancient Egypt. These majestic birds are on the tomb of Nefermaat, who died about 2530 BCE. The soul of the pharaoh was also depicted in the shape of a goose, for just as the goose was seen as the sun emerging from the primeval egg, so the pharaoh was the divine radiance shining upon his people and the whole earth. Indeed part of the ceremonial proclamation of a new pharaoh involved four wild geese being released to fly to the four corners of the earth, so that all the gods would know of the royal good tidings.

In India legend also describes the sun as a golden egg, but in this instance laid by the Great Spirit and from which Brahma, the creator, was born. He is often depicted riding on a goose, his *vahanna* or sacred mount.

The goose was sacred to Wodin, the Norse god of the storms. Geese fly inland when bad weather is brewing, so they were seen as a sign from Wodin that he was on the move.

In classical Greece the goose was sacred to Aphrodite, the goddess of love; but in Rome not to Venus, her counterpart, but to Juno, the goddess of marriage. For Greeks it was a symbol of plenty and fertility. One of Aesop's fables tells of a man who owns a goose that lays golden eggs, a single one each day. Thinking he can get rich more quickly by taking all the eggs within her, he 'kills the goose that laid the golden eggs,' and in so doing ends up by losing everything. George Sand records that in villages in Berry, France, a goose was carried in wedding processions to promote fertility and concord.

On the Atlantic coast of France, the ancient Bretons did not clearly distinguish geese from swans, but held that both were messengers from the underworld, and thus taboo as a food item. And geese were therefore considered fit companions in the graves of Celtic warriors. Julius Caesar was the first foreigner to notice the food taboo and wrote it up in *De Bello Gallico*, his account of his campaigns in Gaul (France) 58 to 50 BCE. British legend added a somber note, claiming that the spring migration of geese was the conducting of damned souls (and, later, of unbaptised infants) to the icy Northern *Hel*, or Hell. While in Wales, the high yapping of (Barnacle) geese passing overhead at night became the *Cwm Anawm*, the Hounds of Hell with their white bodies and red ears. There is a curious link here to the ancient hunting dog of Egypt with its smooth cream body, which now survives only on the Mediterranean island of Ibiza, having been imported there from Carthage, and its pack cry, uncannily similar to that made by Barnacle geese in flight! Yorkshire dialect echoes this, calling geese flying overhead 'gabble-ratchet,' where gabble is a corruption of Gabriel, the archangel, and linked to *gabbras*, a corpse, and uses the medieval word *racche,* the hunting hound that bays for its quarry.

Neither Fish nor Fowl

A bird's scaly legs are a reminder of its reptile ancestors, but it is hard to see any similarity between a goose and a fish. Nevertheless in the Middle Ages during Lent, when fish was permitted to be eaten, a certain species of goose was also allowed on the menu when all other fowl and flesh meats were banned. The justification ran as follows: the Arctic breeding grounds of the Barnacle Goose (*Branta leucopsis*) were unknown to our forbears. The birds left those regions in winter and flew south, alighting on grazing grounds close to the sea. At that time, no one knew about migration either, so it was a mystery how flocks of fully-grown birds could suddenly appear overnight. Searching for a reason, medieval clerics fastened upon an outlandish one in the barnacle – an oddly shaped shell (of the pedunculate genus *Cirripedes*) washed ashore in clusters often attached to driftwood. The long feathery cirri protruding from the valves looked like feathers, a 'beak' fastened the shell to the wood, and the stalks were not unlike the neck of a goose. So did the barnacles produce the geese? Giraldus Cambrensis (1147–1223) embraced this theory, as did the English martyr Edmund Campion (1540–81) in his history of Ireland. So here was an excuse for a more varied Lenten diet: the Barnacle Goose was clearly not fowl but fish! After all, where was the egg? Despite a papal ban by Innocent III in 1215, the practice continued until late into the nineteenth century, at least in western Ireland.

When Pope Pius II visited Scotland in 1468, he tried unsuccessfully to find one of these 'fish birds,' but John Gerrard in his 'The Herball or General Historie of Plantes' (1597) was so convinced of their existence that he went a step further and recorded a 'Goose, or Barnacle Tree' from which by the heat of the sun, geese were said to be born fully fledged. It is reminiscent of Don Alfonso's remark in Mozart's *Cosi fan tutte*: 'like the Arabian phoenix, everyone believes in its existence but no one has ever seen it!'

The Arran Islanders of Scotland always claimed the puffin to be a fish on grounds of its diet and included it in Lenten meals. John Nashe in *Lenten Stuffe* wrote of it quaintly 'half fish, half flesh, a John Indifferent, and an ambodexter between either.'

Goosey, Goosey Gander

Goosey, goosey gander
Whither shall I wander?
Upstairs and downstairs
In my lady's chamber.
There I met an old man
Who wouldn't say his prayers,
So I took him by the left leg
And threw him down the stairs.

Traditional

Nursery rhymes like this one, in the company of fairy tales, myths and legends, are most often attempts either to master in verse form the terror of unknown forces or to control the disguised barbarisms of specific historical events. 'Goosey, Goosey Gander' is no exception.

During the early post-Reformation in sixteenth century England, all Roman Catholics were required to convert to Protestantism. Many refused this undertaking, especially if they were clergy, and as a consequence were mercilessly persecuted by the authorities. 'Recusants' (those who refused to attend Church of England services) were loyal to their priests, whom at great risk they would hide in their homes, especially in 'priest holes' – ingeniously concealed spaces constructed for this specific purpose. In the rhyme it is called 'my lady's chamber,' with reference to Catholic reverence for Mary, 'Our Lady.' The figure of the goose is likely to be a Protestant minister wearing a simple white surplice rather than the colorful Roman vestments. The prayers the Roman Catholic priest refused to intone are the new ones in English, which had replaced the old Latin versions. His obstinacy brings a dire retribution, a probable sentence to be 'hung, drawn, and quartered,' where the victim is taken down 'the stairs' from the scaffold while still alive after hanging, and then eviscerated, before being cut in four pieces and displayed to the crowds.

But rhymes have a long and adaptable life: by the seventeenth century 'Goosey' had taken on satirical overtones – it was the well-known nickname of the mistress of George I, a certain Madame Schulenberg. You could in all innocence chant the rhyme while knowing full well its moral and political implications.

Mother Goose Tales

Fairy tales had been transmitted orally for thousands of years before they were gathered into literary collections. The tales of Mother Goose can be just plausibly traced back to an eighth-century noblewoman, Bertrade of Laon (France). She became Bertrade II on her marriage to Pepin the Short, king of the Franks, and thus became the mother of Charlemagne, founder of the Holy Roman Empire. She was a patroness of children known affectionately as 'Berte aux grand pieds,' which translates into Berthe Bigfoot or Goosefoot! By the seventeenth century the queen had become a bird mother who told charming tales to children.

The first writer to publish fairy tales in the vernacular (classical Greek and Latin stories already existed) was Giovanni Straparola in 1550–53 with his *Delectable Nights* (*Le Piacevoli notti*), the plots of which influenced Shakespeare in such plays as *A Midsummer Night's Dream* and *The Taming of the Shrew,* and before him Edmund Spenser in the *The Faerie Queen.* However, as the Puritans frowned on 'merriment,' the first collection of these tales was made by Charles Perrault in France, in 1697. He entitled it *Histoires ou contes du temps passé* (*Histories or Tales from Times Past*), subtitled *Contes de ma mere l'oye* (*Tales of Mother Goose*), under a charming picture of an old lady storytelling to a group of children and a cat. Many of the tales were his own versions of traditional folktales, and it is these that we recognize today. There is not a tale about Mother Goose herself, but only ones in which a princess is tricked into becoming a goose-girl or gooseherd before being discovered and recovering her true status by a kiss from her Prince Charming.

It was in London's St. Paul's Churchyard in 1744 that John Newbery, bookseller, set up shop and translated and printed an English edition of the fairy tales. Soon after, his stepson Thomas Carnan first published a book of traditional rhymes and so-called nonsense songs under the title *Mother Goose's Melody; or Sonnets from the Cradle*.

The history of Mother Goose in the United States begins with these rhymes under the same title in 1786, the year before the Constitution was drawn up in Philadelphia, when an official and noteworthy book (unlike the pirated editions then current) came from the presses of Isaiah Thomas in Boston. The songs included such favorites as 'Little Tommy Tucker' and 'Jack and Jill.' The story put about in 1860 that it had been in 1719 that Thomas Fleet published S*ongs for the Nursery or Mother Goose's Melodies for Children* has no substance despite the fact that he did marry an Elizabeth Goose and that no doubt her mother sang songs to her grand-child. Whatever false claims, the following words from one of the pirated versions ring true:

> No, No, my Melodies will never die
> While nurses sing or babies cry.

The Goose Bible

When Mary Tudor briefly ruled England (1553–58), her reign introduced a new wave of persecution, this time against the Protestants, many of whom fled the country. Geneva was a preferred refuge not only because it had a Protestant govern-ment but also because it was close to the great print works of Germany. The refugees enjoyed the freedom to publish their religious views and, in particular, to print Bibles in English, not in the prescribed Latin, continuing the pioneering English translations of the reformers William Tyndale and Miles Coverdale.

Most were editions of the great Geneva Bible, the work of the exiles Antony Gilby, William Whittingham, and Thomas Sampson. One of these was printed in 1560 in the town of Dort (Dortrecht in Holland). The Dort Press had as its trademark a goose and hence the title, 'The Goose Bible.' These were the first of the Bibles in English to be small in size, printed in roman type, with the chapters divided into verses, and the first in which italics were used for explanatory and connective words. The Goose Bible went into 200 known editions and eventually acquired a popular name, 'The Breeches Bible,' because in its version of Genesis 3:7 the translator wrote of Adam and Eve that 'the eyes of them both were opened . . . and they sowed figge-tree leaves together and made themselves breeches.'

Bird of the Saints

Legends associate at least three saints with geese: St. Werburga of Chester and St. Hilda of Whitby, and St. Martin of Tours. St. Martin, who lived in fourth-century Gaul, was allegedly so reluctant to leave his hermit life to become bishop of Tours that, when summoned to his consecration, he hid himself in a barn full of geese. True to form the geese raised the alarm and Martin was discovered. But to recompense him for taking office, the new bishop was offered a feast of goose and ever after the goose has been associated with him and eaten on his feast day, Martinmas, the 11th of November. Most of us associate St. Martin with generosity more than with geese, especially his act of dividing his cloak with a beggar. His reputation for saintliness was such that his cloak, in late Latin/Italian *capella*, was housed in his shrine at Tours, which became a place of veneration for the Frankish kings (who took the cloak with them into battle) and for pilgrims on their way to Santiago de Compostela. In fact St. Martin's *capella* inspired our word 'chapel,' a holy place of prayer.

Goose on the Menu . . .

The Greeks kept domesticated geese, and in the *Odyssey*, Penelope fed and fattened a flock of 20 on soaked grain. The Romans, too, enjoyed the roast bird, dividing it up according to the status of the consumer, the front part for the master and his family, the back portions for the servants. Then as now the lucky person got the 'wishbone' (breastbone) which, held between the hands, had the power to grant any wish, a superstition no doubt derived from a primitive form of augury. It is reported that Queen Elizabeth was eating goose on September 29, 1588, when she heard her navy had defeated the Spanish Armada. Had she been given the wishbone that day?

But it was the Roman practical (and cruel) genius that discovered *pâté de foie gras*, a potted meat made from goose liver, enlarged by force-feeding the creature with a mixture of milk, wheat, or maize flour, and honey. The Roman practice was to confine the geese in a small space, sometimes with their feet nailed to the ground, and to feed them 6 pounds of the mixture a day, equivalent to an intake for us of 28 pounds of cooked spaghetti! The taste and torture required for the pâté seemed to decline for many centuries before reappearing in southwest France and also in the Alsace.

The meat of these overfed geese is, in fact, tough – and so clever cooks devised the art of the *confit*: rubbed with garlic and covered in rough salt, goose pieces are left for hours until softened, then cooked in goose fat with onions for a further three hours before being packed in stoneware jars with more goose fat.

The great doyen of French provincial cooking, Elizabeth

David, recounts that when her friend the English writer Norman Douglas (1869–1952) was told that the Greeks regarded goose fat as an aphrodisiac, he was determined to test this thesis for himself, only to discover not an enhancement to romance but a very effective emetic! The Greeks did use it successfully for skin complaints. And in France even today it is used in rural areas to relieve chesty colds.

Fat from kosher-slaughtered geese (or chicken) was the staple cooking medium for observant Jews of Eastern Europe and the Rhineland, instead of the more common, but non-kosher, pork fat. It was called *schmaltz* or *shmaltz*, a word that later became synonymous with excessive (dripping) sentimentality. Despite medical opinion that fat is bad for you, the goose-rearing areas of the France have the lowest incidence of heart disease, and chemical analysis has shown the fat's properties to be akin to olive oil.

At the end of the nineteenth century, as winter approached, for warmth poor children in the slums of London were rubbed all over with goose fat, padded out with newspaper for insulation, and then sewn into their clothes. Lice and fleas had a field day until the 'Spring Clean,' when the children could once again take off their clothes.

The Useful Goose

'Last night I slept in a goose-feather bed,' sings the girl in the song 'The Raggle-Taggle Gypsies, O.' She is recalling the comforts of the home she has left. For hundreds of years goose feathers provided the bedding that was part of a girl's dowry. Little girls were expected 'to pluck for their wedding' as soon as they were able to.

> Cackle, cackle, Mother Goose,
> Have you any feathers loose?
> Truly have I, pretty fellow,

Half enough to fill a pillow.
Here are quills, take one or two,
And down to make a bed for you.

Traditional

The feathers were graded, the top being the soft breast down, used by the bird itself to line its nest and cover its eggs. The best were used for the pillows and quilts and the coarser for the mattress. Even nowadays, the duvets with the highest 'tog ratings' (measurement of warmth) are those made from goose down.

The long wing feathers, or 'quills,' were used for writing before the steel pen was invented. The word 'pen' is also the name for a female goose, 'cob' being the male. The French were less specific, using the neutral *plume*, meaning feather, when naming their pen (although it is a feminine word). The whole wing was used as a broom, which wing depended on whether you were right- or left-handed.

At one time the goose was highly regarded in yet another art, that of steelmaking. As long ago as the fifth century, the Franks used to blend iron filings with flour and feed this mixture to their geese. Goose manure is rich in carbon and nitrogen, and the iron-enriched droppings were used as a toughening agent in the forging of steel blades.

The Watchful Goose

The high haunting call of wild geese above the noise of wind and waves is a thrilling sound that makes the heart leap; but the clamor made by domestic geese mercilessly jars on the ear, and for that very reason can be most useful. In 1986 the American 32nd Army Air Defense Command paid almost 25,000 dollars for 900 guards for their 30 air defense installations in West Germany. These were neither security personnel nor Alsatian dogs, but geese. Geese are less expensive to maintain, make effective alarm systems, and with their 25- to 40-year lifespan give long service. A gander in Lancashire, England, known as George, died in 1976 at the age of 49 years and 8 months!

Chaucer, in his *Parlemente of Fowles* (1382), included no less than 43 wild birds, an invaluable source of our avian knowledge of the period. Besides naming them, he gave each a shorthand description, and it is significant that he gave to the goose the epithet 'waker,' or 'watchful.' Michael Drayton (1563–1631) is another who emphasized this particular trait of the goose by dating it back to the patriarchs of the Bible in his poem *Noah's Flood*:

> The goose which doth for watchfulness excel
> Came for the rest to be the sentinel.

The Romans certainly knew the goose's security value. In 390 BCE the Gauls attacked Rome. As the invaders stealthily climbed up the Capitoline Hill by night, the Roman garrison under Marcus Manlius was alerted by the cackle of the sacred geese kept in the precincts of the Temple of Juno. The attack was repulsed, the city saved and, to commemorate the event, a golden goose – a real goose dressed in gold – was paraded each year in procession. At the same time a dog was sacrificed as a punishment and warning to all watchdogs not to fail in their duty.

Driven Geese

Along the ancient pathways on the ridges above the forests of Britain, long before the Romans came, men would drive cattle, sheep, pigs, and also geese to market. These men were called 'drovers,' tough, weathered men, armed and ready for any eventuality, at times having to travel hundreds of miles. (Much later, the cowboys of the American West were their worthy successors, marshaling those enormous cattle drives to the railheads, to take the livestock to the abattoirs of the industrial cities of the North.) The journeys were long and arduous and so to protect the feet of the geese, the birds were first driven through a mixture of tar, sawdust, and sand. (Nothing so basic for pigs, which were treated to woollen booties, nor for turkeys shod in leather.) In flocks of sometimes over 20,000, the geese were driven for weeks to the great goose fairs of the land such as that at Nottingham, which lasted 21 days and whose existence long predated its formal status granted in 1541. Tavistock Goosey Fair in Devon is still held, and although geese are in short supply, goose pies are still on sale.

The droves started out, mainly from the counties of Lincolnshire, Norfolk, and Suffolk, and the West Country, in August, when the harvest was almost completed. They fed on the stubble fields on the way, reaching their destination just before Michaelmas, the feast day of St. Michael and all Angels, the 29th of September, when roast goose was the traditional fare.

Geese can average only 1.25 mph, a very slow rate of progress, and so experiments to replace them with other, speedier birds were attempted. In 1740 the marquess of Queensbury (famous patron of the turf, whose descendant invented the rules of boxing) had a bet with another nobleman that a flock of turkeys would walk to London in a shorter time than a flock of geese. But he lost. Geese grazed by the wayside as they walked while the turkeys had to stop to be fed. Turkeys also roosted in trees at night and had to be persuaded to come down in the morning, while the geese just followed their gander.

On Terms with Geese

'A wild goose chase' means a futile search and originated in Elizabethan times when it was a game of 'follow the leader' on horseback. Samuel Johnson in his *Dictionary of the English Language* (1755) defined it as 'a pursuit of something as unlikely to be caught as a wild goose.'

If a player gets a 'goose egg' in any sport, his score is nil. The egg as a symbol of '0,' or zero, turns up again in the tennis term 'love,' a possible corruption of the French word *l'oeuf,* which means egg. In the English game of cricket, a score of naught is called 'a duck,' short for duck's egg.

When a goose is plucked, its skin is covered in the raised pimples where the feather shafts had been. So to have 'goose-flesh' or 'goose pimples' is to have a skin covered in minute bumps due to cold or fear. 'Even my goose pimples have got goose pimples!' said the terrified Bob Hope in one of his film comedy roles.

Geese were thought of as stupid, nervous creatures (the Latin writer Ovid disagreed – he called the goose 'wiser than a dog'); 'Don't be a silly goose!' is a common rebuke, and we say of a timid person that 'he can't say boo to a goose.' A favorite subject for medieval wood carvings in churches was a fox dressed up as a monk preaching to a flock of geese, the moral being 'Don't be gullible!' And the phrase 'everything is lovely and the goose hangs high' signifies the bird is plucked and out of reach of the wily fox.

The 'royal game of goose,' mentioned in the Irish-born English writer Oliver Goldsmith's long poem *The Deserted Village* (1770), is a board game of ancient lineage, with strong links to labyrinth puzzles and symbolism. Francesco de Medici had reinvented it in Renaissance Florence and it became popular in Tudor England in the late sixteenth century. It is supposed to represent a kind of 'Pilgrim's Progress' of life to death and is played like the English board game 'Snakes and Ladders.' *Jeu de l'oie* (Goose Game), on the other hand, was a gambling game in France and a favorite with Napoleon.

'To get the bird' is to be hissed (like a goose) off a stage, so we find that in Victorian times 'to goose' was to express extreme displeasure in the world of musicals and dramatic shows. In Charles Dickens's *Hard Times* Mr. Gradgrind is informed of the sorry lot of poor Jupe, the elderly clown of Sleary's Circus Ring: 'He was goosed last night, he was goosed the night before, and he was goosed today.' The sorry fellow had mistimed his tips (leaps), and was loose in his ponging (tumbling). The circus public were unforgiving.

'To goose someone' is a slang expression meaning to prod or pinch them playfully on the behind. The verb probably comes from the jabbing of a goose's bill. Noel Coward sang a lyric about a merry widow on holiday called Mrs. Wentworth-Brewster. In a bar on the island of Capri three young Italian sailors from Messina bowed to Mrs. Wentworth-Brewster, said 'Scusi,' and promptly 'goosed her.' It created a lively scene.

Journey of the Snow Geese

In spring the Snow Goose (*Chen caerulescens*) migrates from the southern states of the U.S. and northern Mexico on a 3,000-mile journey to its breeding grounds in the Canadian Arctic. In their U-formations, flying at 60 miles an hour and at a height of up to 8,000 feet and numbering in the millions, it is a wondrous journey, across the Great Plains, over boreal conifer forests and open tundra. Then to Hudson Bay, crossing the vast expanse of water until reaching Baffin Island, where they will spread across the Arctic.

7

The Kingfisher

A flash of blue and white along a stream, an orange streak breaking the water's surface, and that may well be your only sighting of the kingfisher. This flying jewel or, as the poet Tennyson put it, 'the secret splendour of the brooks,' is the Belted Kingfisher, the only common kingfisher in North America. Kingfishers alternate between perching quite still for long periods of time (often preening their feathers after a dive) and suddenly exploding into action.

The kingfisher comes in various forms. The order of birds Coraciiformes has nine families, of which the kingfishers are found in the suborder Alcedines.

All kingfishers are birds of prey, but their dietary requirements are varied: for many the main staple of their diet is fish, but at least 66 species are not aquatic but rather dry-land dwellers, and their mainly insect diet features such delicacies as flies, moths, centipedes, and even earthworms. The last are the particular fancy of the Shovel-billed Kingfisher, a large and swollen-billed specimen, who literally 'plows' a square meter of soil, thrashing the earth with a side-to-side motion of his beak in order to turn up grubs and worms, which he tugs up with an enthusiasm worthy of a thrush.

Two other kingfishers exhibit even more extraordinary table manners: the Kookaburra seizes a snake, carries it to a good height, then drops it so that it falls and stuns itself, ready for consumption. And the Ruddy Kingfisher of the Philippines prepares large land snails for its palate by smashing them on 'anvil' stones, again like the thrush. Spiders, insects, grass-hoppers, crustacea, even scorpions, mice, and skinks are prey to different kingfishers as well as their more familiar diet of fish.

The color spectrum of the kingfisher is remarkable. The small Oriental Dwarf Kingfisher (*Ceyx erithacus*) of Indonesia, for example, is red. The Red-breasted Paradise Kingfisher (*Tanysiptera nympha*) has an orange bill. The Mountain Yellow-billed Kingfisher (*Halcyon megarhyncha*) is an inhabitant of the high forests of New Guinea. Kingfishers of the Pacific and of the Americas come in dazzling shades of green, and are liberally splashed with blue, indigo, violet, and purple.

A French Legend

Noah sent the dove out from the ark to search for signs of receding rain and, growing impatient for the dove's return, sent the kingfisher as well. This doughty little bird soon flew straight into a storm and, struck by lightning, was striped from head to tail a brilliant blue. Undeterred, it flew higher to overcome the storm but its path brought it too near the sun, which, for its impertinence, singed its breast and, as the poor bird turned to flee, its rump was singed as well! When the kingfisher returned to earth, the flood was gone and so was the ark, together with its captain.

So, it was said, the kingfisher still flies up and down streams in search of Noah and the ark.

A superstition has it that hanging the feather of a blue kingfisher around your neck protects you from the fire of lightning.

Halcyon Days

Halcyon is the kingfisher's poetic name and it links the bird to the sea. According to a classical legend, Alcyone, the daughter of Oceanus (or Aeolus), had power over the wind and was blissfully married to Ceyx, son of the Morning Star. Zeus, jealous of her marriage and power over the wind, killed Ceyx by hurling a thunderbolt at the vessel in which he was sailing, drowning him in the shipwreck. Distraught, Alcyone threw herself into the sea, to join her husband in his watery grave, but Zeus, repenting of his churlish act, turned them both into kingfishers. Many sailors, with the legend in mind, have regarded the halcyon bird, or kingfisher, as their protector from storms and rough passage. The bird was believed to nest seven days before and after the winter solstice and to brood her eggs on a nest of fish bones, which floated on the sea. These days of tranquility and complete peace were called 'the halcyon days.'

Basil the Great, an ancient preacher and bishop of Caesarea from 370 to 379, told the legend in a different way to make a pious homily of it:

> The halcyon is a sea bird which nests by the shore, laying its eggs in the sand and bringing forth its young in the middle of winter when the sea beats against the land in violent and frequent storms. But during the seven days while the halcyon broods (for it takes seven days to hatch its young) all the winds sink to rest and the sea grows calm. And as it then is in need of food for its young ones, the most bountiful God grants this little creature another seven days of calm that it may feed its young. Since all sailors know this,

they give this time the name of the halcyon days. These things are ordered by the providence of God for the creatures that are without reason that you may be led to seek of God the things you need of God for your own salvation. And, when for this small bird, he holds back the great and fearful sea, and bids it be calm in winter, what will he not do for you made in his own image? And if he so tenderly cherish the halcyon, how much more will he not give you when you call on him with all your heart?

'As Kingfishers Catch Fire'

Gerard Manley Hopkins used the kingfisher and the dragonfly to laud the fact that all creatures are to be just themselves. We ourselves are created to be just ourselves:

As kingfishers catch fire, dragonflies draw flame;
As tumbled over rim in roundy wells
Stones ring; like each tucked string tells, each hung bell's
Bow swung finds tongue to fling out broad its name;
Each mortal thing does one thing and the same:
Deals out that being indoors each one dwells;
Selves – goes itself; *myself* it speaks and spells,
Crying *What I do is me: for that I came.*

Gerard Manley Hopkins (1844–89)

8

The Ostrich

Amazingly, the ostrich has survived all its predators – including humans – in spite of being flightless. Its basic advantage is that it is the largest bird in the world and is possessed of an enviable mobility. As early as the fourth century BCE, Xenophon, general and historian, was reporting 'an ostrich no one succeeded in catching; those horsemen who hunted the bird soon desisted from the pursuit, for it far outstripped them in its flight, using its feet for running, and its wings, raising them like a sail.'

A Victorian explorer, Joseph Thomson, arriving in Tanganyika (Tanzania) in 1882, some 25 years after his more famous predecessor, Richard Burton, wrote of 'troops of ostriches scudding away out of danger . . . too wary for the stalker.' It is also a fierce opponent when aroused. It uses its legs, feet, and beak in the attack, kicking like a kangaroo forwards, not backwards like a horse, employing its strongly nailed toe to lethal effect, while all the time making a low-key, lion-like roaring sound. It has been known to kick a fully grown lion to death.

When Is a Bird Not a Bird?

It neither flies nor sings – can it be a bird? Even the appearance of the ostrich seems to come from the drawing board of a wayward cartoonist, not from the hand of the Creator. Carl von Linne, the Swedish Count (Linnaeus) who classified all birds, struggled to find words to describe it and ended with its classical name, *Struthio camelus*, 'bird-camel' or 'ostrich-camel' (the classical Greeks, even more baffled, called it 'the large sparrow'). Linnaeus found the resemblances in its long neck and legs, large protuberant eyes and love of a dry, open habitat, but in little else.

A Long History

There is evidence that 12 million years ago the ostrich had a widespread distribution in India, China, Greece, and into Africa.

In the third millennium BCE, in Egypt, the ostrich was a familiar sight and held in high regard. An ostrich feather played an essential role in the soul's journey in the afterlife. At death, the soul or *ba* was conducted into the hall of judgement by the god Horus where the person's heart, the seat of conscience, was weighed on scales counter-balanced by the ostrich feather. The feather represented justice, righteousness, and truth, for all such feathers were held to be of equal length and weight. If the balance was found equal, the soul and the spirit united to go into eternal bliss; if not, a monster devoured the heart, while the soul entered a perpetual sleep. In sculptured bas-reliefs of that time, pharaohs were often shown holding a fan of ostrich feathers to demonstrate the fairness of their rule.

Royal Feathers

The ostrich feather was once a fashionable accessory. It made a highly publicized comeback with the commemorative fan of three pure white feathers made for the marriage of Charles, Prince of Wales, and Lady Diana Spencer on July 29, 1981. For more than six hundred years, a crest of three white ostrich feathers and the motto 'Ich Dien' ('I serve') has been the badge of each succeeding Prince of Wales. At the battle of Crecy in 1346, the blind king of Bohemia died fighting for the French against the English. It is said that when the battle was over, the victorious English King Edward III awarded the three-feathered crest of the blind king to his own 16-year-old son, the Black Prince, for having fought so bravely. The same device turns up in many places, especially as a pub sign, 'The Feathers,' and on the reverse of the British two-pence coin.

The Tale of an Egg

Alongside the ostrich's amazing durability, we find a wealth of mythical and symbolic associations. For instance, there was a belief that the hen ostrich hatched her eggs by just gazing at them, with love.

Robert Southey refers to this in his poem 'Thalaba':

> Oh! Even with such a look as fables say
> The mother ostrich fixes on her eggs,
> Till that intense affection
> Kindle the light of life.
>
> Robert Southey (1774–1843)

Simultaneously, if she took her eyes off the eggs for one second, they would become addled. The belief was used as an image of God's constant loving care for humankind without which we would become lifeless.

The ostrich egg itself, being the largest known to humans, became a symbol of the creation, for many belief systems had the Primeval Egg as the source of all things created. So also by association it became a symbol of fertility and of the hidden nature of life before it becomes visible at birth. Philo made a direct relation between this idea and the roasted egg eaten by Jews as part of the Passover meal, commemorating the Exodus from Egypt and their rebirth as a nation. (It was also the rebirth of the year at springtime.)

The Easter egg is a continuation of this, symbolizing the burial and resurrection of Jesus, a new birth and new creation. From the Middle Ages, church inventories mention placing an ostrich egg on the altar at Easter and other holy days. Today in Coptic churches this is still the practice. In the Spanish city of Burgos, in the cathedral, an ostrich egg is placed at the feet of the crucified Christ.

Head in the Sand

The ostrich is notoriously difficult to observe at close quarters. This could explain the persistent mistaken belief that when the bird is frightened, it buries its head in the sand. We accuse someone who is afraid of facing unpleasant facts as behaving like an ostrich. Thomas More wrote:

> Whole nations fooled by falsehood, fear or pride,
> Their ostrich heads in self-delusion hide.
>
> Thomas More (1478–1535)

Despite its established usage, the observation is incorrect. The ostrich does not bury its head in the sand when danger threatens. It sinks to the ground, and stretches out its neck, so that it merges with the contours of the landscape.

The Unkindest Cut of All

The actual physical characteristics of the ostrich always seemed to cause offence: their incongruity gave rise to some odd, and often unpleasant notions. In the book of Lamentations we find the following:

> Even whales uncover the teat
> And suckle their young;
> But the daughters of my people are cruel
> As ostriches in the desert.
>
> Lamentations 4:3

And the author of the book of Job continues the calumny with a whole list of supposed wrongdoing:

> The wings of the ostrich are stunted;
> Her pinions and plumage are so scanty
> That she abandons her eggs to the ground,
> Letting them be kept warm by the sand.
> She forgets that a foot may crush them,
> Or a wild beast trample on them;
> She treats her chicks heartlessly as if they were not hers,
> Not caring if her labour is wasted
> (for God has denied her wisdom
> and left her without sense),
> While like a cock she stuts over the uplands,
> Scorning both horse and rider.
>
> Job 39:13–18

St. Gregory the Great made no refutation of these slanders but rather added to them, when he was writing advice to his monks on their spiritual problems. As was his custom, he drew illustrations from nature:

What is designated by the word 'ostriches,' but those who pretend that they are good, retain a life of sanctity in appearance, as a wing for flight, but use it not in act.

St. Gregory saw the ostrich as going against the natural order of creation by its flightlessness and used it to illustrate the hypocritical behavior of some of his monks, whose outward and visible signs did not match an inward and spiritual reality.

In fact, ostriches pair for life and are model parents, however many chicks are produced, and have evolved naturally to their state of flightlessness. But neither the biblical authors nor their early commentators were zoologists writing natural histories. They understood their purpose as the teaching of spiritual reality. If the flora and fauna of the Bible provided the means to this end, they would make from them valid spiritual points.

Ostrich Digest

The ostrich, that will eat
A horseshoe so great,
In the stead of meat,
Such fervent heat
His stomach doth freat [gnaw].

John Skelton (ca. 1460–1529)

The ostrich is listed among the 'unclean' creatures of the Jewish Bible – deemed unfit to eat. Although existing on a mainly vegetarian diet, it is partial to the odd lizard or snake and hence, possibly, the reason for the ban. Also, some other very strange things have been found in the ostrich's stomach – barbed wire, bullets, stones, and pieces of wood, to mention a few. Fifty-three diamonds were discovered in one surprisingly discriminate bird. But the collection that most defies belief was that found during an autopsy on an ostrich at the

London Zoo. In its stomach were found an alarm clock, three feet of rope, a spool of film, a cycle valve, three gloves, a comb, a handkerchief, and an unspecified number of coins and paper clips.

Shakespeare sided with John Skelton and had one of his characters say in *Henry VI, Part II*, 'But I'll make thee eat iron like an ostrich, and swallow my great sword like a pin, 'ere thou and I part.' And we still talk of someone having 'a stomach like an ostrich.'

Onwards and Upwards

The eating habits of the ostrich, together with its odd looks, could account for its historically low place in our human estimation of creatures. But there is another less obvious reason. A deep-rooted dream of the human psyche has been the longing 'to fly like a bird,' so well expressed in the myth of Icarus, the man who mastered flight but flew too near the sun, so that the wax holding his wings melted and he fell back to earth – a fatal lesson in *hubris*, the Greek word for that overweening pride that attracted the wrath of the gods. While the heroes and gods of the Greeks, such as Perseus or Hermes, strapped into their winged sandals, could fly the skies with impunity, humankind remained earthbound. Our best endeavors, even those of Leonardo da Vinci, failed, at least until the Wright brothers lifted us skywards in their flying machines. We cannot fly independently, so it offends us that any bird should willingly relinquish this enviable skill.

9

The Owl

Over the ages and across many cultures and countries, the owl has met with a mixed and often contradictory popular reception. Venerated by some and feared by others, the owl has often been treated with suspicion and fright and associated with the dark side of our life – with death and doom and evil. A creature of the night, of dark habits and shining eyes, with a ghostly, sometimes strident voice and silent flight, the bird makes foul nests in ruins, hollow trees and holes, and being a bird that preys on unthreatening small mammals, the owl has unintentionally been author of its own sinister reputation. Indeed, in human imagination, the owl became a harbinger of death and a source of malignancy.

Another tradition endowed the order Strigiformes with wisdom and patience and aligned it with immortality. The ornithological studies of the eighteenth century and their scientific observations replaced much of the superstition that surrounded the owl, until today it is generally regarded with affection, and there is a care and concern for its conservation.

Owls are divided into two families, Barn Owls and Typical Owls, and there are over 150 species with an amazing range of appearance, habitats, and habits. Size matters enormously in the identification of species: the tiny Elf Owl is so minute that it breeds in holes drilled in cacti by woodpeckers; the bulky Great Horned Owl can kill skunks and grouse; and the Great Gray Owl, our largest owl (which is also found in Northern Europe and Asia), is up to 30 inches long, but weighs as little as 2 pounds because of the thick down that covers its body.

The Wise Owl

Two formal Owls together sat,
Conferring thus in solemn chat:
How is the modern taste decay'd!
Where's the respect to wisdom paid?
Our worth the Grecian sages knew:
They gave our sires the honour due;
They weighed the dignity of fowls,
And pry'd into the depth of Owls.
Athens the seat of learned fame,
With general voice revered our name;
On merit, title was conferr'd,
And all adored the Athenian bird.

John Gay (1685–1732)

The Greeks worshiped Athena, the goddess of war and of wisdom; her favorite creature was the owl, which replaced the crow as her consort (wisdom before wiliness), and consequently owls were once held sacred in Athens. Athena's owl was the Little Owl (*Athene noctua*) which was introduced into England in the nineteenth century by Lord Lilford. It has a fierce frowning face and, despite its Latin name, which means 'night,' can often be seen in the daylight perched on telephone wires or poles. Perhaps its association with Athena derived from the intensity of its gaze, unblinking and still, and looking out of disproportionately large eyes that appear full of all knowledge. Athena was often called 'the grey-eyed one' or 'Athena of the shining orbs.'

These owls were so abundant in Athens that the Athenians had a saying, 'Don't send owls to Athens,' the equivalent of our 'coals to Newcastle.' The Athenians were the first people to use double-sided coins. On one side was Athena – or Pallas Athena, so named after one of her legendary conquests – and on the other her owl, obviously to supervise the Greeks' trade and commerce, the staple of their empire. The coins were known as 'owls.' They were in circulation in Greece for hundreds of years, and all European coinage developed from them.

At the well-preserved Roman baths in Bath, England, we find that beside a statue of Minerva, the Latin equivalent of Athena, there is a delightfully sculpted figure of an owl, proof that she retained the attributes of her Greek divine forebear.

In the Christian tradition also, the owl was used to represent wisdom. In a painting by Cosima Tura (1431–95) we discover St. Jerome translating the Bible into Latin and on a tree behind him is perched an owl, the symbol of the wisdom of this great scholar. Jerome's translation, called the 'Vulgate' ('for the ordinary people'), was completed in about 404 CE. His scholarship became the byword for wisdom, his Bible becoming the official version used by the church until the Reformation, confirmed as the orthodox translation for the Roman church by the Council of Trent in 1546.

In 1850, a Little Owl fell out of her nest above the pillars of the Parthenon in Athens and was attacked by a gang of Athenian youths, who no longer regarded the bird as sacred. The boys scattered when a stern female voice rebuked them. This formidable English tourist rescued the owl and nursed it back to health at her home at Embley in Hampshire. The bird, which she appropriately called 'Athena,' became so tame that its mistress carried it around in the deep pocket of her dress. That lady was Florence Nightingale.

Owl-lovers

Through language and literature children are still brought up to believe in the owl's wisdom. Women in charge of packs of junior Girl Guides, or Brownies, are known as 'Brown Owl,' a reassuring title that suggests experience and understanding. 'Old Brown' is the awe-inspiring owl in Beatrix Potter's *The Tale of Squirrel Nutkin*. To stay on the right side of this intimidating bird, the squirrels keep bringing him little offerings including 'three fat mice' and 'a fine fat mole.' And there is 'Owl' in A. A. Milne's *Winnie the Pooh* stories, highly respected by all the inhabitants of 'Ten Acre Wood' for his skill in reading and writing (a status perhaps unwarranted since he can only spell his own name W-O-L).

A romantic bird rather than a wise one is how one would describe the risks taken by that odd couple, the Owl and the Pussycat, in Edward Lear's affectionate poem of that title. Their long, briny courtship in the precarious pea green boat, their somewhat extempore marital arrangements with the Pig and the Turkey on the island where the Bong-tree grows, and their unhealthy diet of endless spoonfuls of quince, combine to make them a very strange pair indeed.

The Owl and the Pussycat do, however, have some likenesses. The owl has been described as a cat with wings. It is adept at hunting small rodents. They both watch silently and strike quickly. The owl, like the cat, can be noisy during the night, disturbing the peace with raucous courting screams and shouts. They are both regarded affectionately by many people. A sign of the affection for owls is their extraordinary popularity as toys – second, possibly, only to teddy bears. Partly their attraction is their erect posture, and partly those two large eyes looking so intently and alertly.

Many cultures consider the owl in a kindly light. Australia's Aborigines believe that owls are the spirits of women and are therefore sacred. The Inuit of the Arctic consider them a good source of guidance and make pets of them; the Hopi of the Southwest see the Burrowing Owl as god of their dead and nurturer of all underground events including seed germination; while the Great Horned Owl was believed to help their peaches grow. The Tlingit of Alaska had such confidence in the owl that they would rush into battle hooting their war cries, and the Incas of South America venerated them. In Samoa, all people are believed to descend from the owl, their common ancestor, while the Ainu of Japan held the Fish Owl in particular esteem as possessing a divinity benevolent to their fishing needs.

The Mongols particularly revered the owl. Genghis Khan hid from his enemies under a bush on which an owl was perched. His pursuers thought that it was impossible that he could be concealed in such a place. Therefore his followers honored the owl as his protector.

The Owl's Eyes

The owl's eyesight is called tubular and is adapted to low light intensity. The greatly enlarged and, relatively speaking, enormous lens and iris of the eye trap the utmost possible light. Those huge eyes mean that owls are particularly adapted to night hunting. They have only binocular vision, that is the ability to focus (as opposed to being able to search widely), and this in a mere arc of 90 degrees as their eyes are too large in their sockets to move. As a result, the owl's whole head has to rotate and it can actually turn its head through 270 degrees and look backwards. Most birds enjoy a high visual resolution enabling them to see clearly, but owls have exceptionally high sensitivity, being able to record ten times more than humans. So they can detect even the slightest movement on the ground beneath them.

They also possess very acute hearing, an advantage aided by the special facial feather tufts on either side of their head,

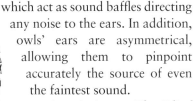

which act as sound baffles directing any noise to the ears. In addition, owls' ears are asymmetrical, allowing them to pinpoint accurately the source of even the faintest sound.

A painting – *The Blind Fiddler* by Cornelius Bega, dated to 1663, in the Ashmolean Museum in Oxford – shows an owl (in a print or drawing) in the background. The artist probably thought, as was mistakenly supposed at that time, that the owl suffered blindness and was therefore a fit symbol of human struggles, suggesting a moral to the painting.

St. Eustathius saw the owl's eyesight in a different light. He thought that the owl's eyes dissolved shadows and thus enabled it to see clearly at night. This he compared with the all-seeing vision of Jesus Christ.

Two Legends

Two legends condemn the owl for having a mean streak. The first is a traditional French story that explains the owl's aversion to daylight. When the little wren first brought fire from heaven to earth, he scorched his plumage. All the birds offered a feather in gratitude, except the owl, who said he needed all his feathers to keep himself warm. The birds condemned his selfishness and told him that from then on he would spend all his days alone and would always suffer from the cold at night. That is why, the story tells, owls sleep by day, hunt by night,

and always fluff up their feathers, because they are perpetually cold. John Keats draws on the French legend.

> St. Agnes' Eve – Ah bitter chill it was!
> The owl, for all its feathers, was a-cold.
>
> *The Eve of St. Agnes* by John Keats (1795–1821)

The second legend is an old Gloucestershire one concerning
Jesus and a baker's daughter. Jesus comes into a bakery for
something to eat. The baker's wife puts a cake in the oven for
him, but the daughter declares it too large and cuts it in half.
The diminished dough rises to an enormous size and the
greedy girl promptly turns into an owl. In Shakespeare's
Hamlet, Ophelia's otherwise curious line 'they say the owl
was a baker's daughter' is thus explained.

The Bird of Ill Repute

The symbolic language of birds has never been logical, and
human reactions to particular birds have often been contradictory. The owl is a good example of the way in which our imagination has seen the bird in darker or lighter shades. In many
ancient cultures it was seen as a creature of darkness. It was an
evil omen, a bearer of bad news, and a prophet of doom. Many
people believed owls to be messengers of witches and sorcer-
ers. It was linked with our natural fears of the night.

The Chinese called it 'the bird which snatches away the
soul'; the Apache claimed 'when the owl hoots, the Indian
dies'; and we find a Canadian Indian tribe with the same idea
in Margaret Craven's book *I Heard the Owl Call My Name*,
where she writes, enigmatically, 'The Village [of the tribe] is
the talking bird, the owl, who calls the name of the man who
is going to die. . . .' The idea persisted into relatively modern
times, and John Bourke, in his book *Apache Campaign in the
Sierra Nevada*, relates how Apache scouts tracking Geronimo

were so terrified by a captured owl that they refused to continue until the bird was left behind.

The superstitious Romans were very leery of owls (witches could turn themselves into owls, some Romans believed) so that whenever one was seen in Rome, the city had to be purified to rid it of the bird's supposedly malign influence. In the Egypt of the pharaohs, the owl could be very bad news indeed, for when the pharaoh had no further need of a minister, he would send him an image of the bird, signifying death. This was a hint that he was now expected to do the gentlemanly thing and dispose of himself. Diodorus Siculus tells of a mother who, with her own hands, strangled her son who was too cowardly to perform the necessary act of suicide himself. The same custom prevailed in Ethiopia. The condemned person knew what he had to do when he was shown an owl painted on a table.

The 'evil messenger' characteristic of the owl found further expression in Renaissance Europe. Chaucer called the owl the prophet of 'wo and misschaunce'; Spenser referred to it as 'death's dreadful messenger.' Later, Shakespeare followed suit. In *Macbeth*, just before the murder of Duncan, Lady Macbeth speaks of the bird as portending death: 'the owl has shrieked, the fatal bellman which gives the stern'st goodnight.' In *Julius Caesar*, the appearance of an owl in daytime (signifying the break up of the natural order in both nature and the state) foretold the assassination and death of the emperor:

> . . . the bird of night did sit
> Even at noonday upon the market place,
> Hooting and shrieking . . .

Elsewhere Shakespeare calls it 'the boding scritch owl' and 'the ominous and fearful owl of death.' In *Henry VI, Part III* is the line 'The owl shrieked at my birth, an evil sign.' Up to the nineteenth century, farmers in Britain would nail an owl to the barn door to ward off evil. Even to this day, people of the Shetland Islands regard the owl as destructive, capable of tainting cows' milk with blood, even of killing the beast if it brushes against it.

The Christian church, too, was a party to this same attitude and in its iconography the owl was almost always a symbol of ignorance and evil. To support this, there was the rabbinical tradition that Adam's first wife was called Lilith, a synonym for death, but translated in some versions of the tale as 'owl' (or sometimes as 'night-monster'), who was subsequently dispossessed by Eve, source of life, and banished to the nether regions.

A Voice Legend

A Spanish legend excuses the owl for his harsh voice with a touching tale of compassion for Christ. Before the crucifixion the owl was the sweetest of singers, but so shocked was he at the sight of Jesus hanging on the tree, the owl has ever since shunned the daylight and now only ever repeats the words '*Cruz, Cruz*' ('Cross, Cross').

Tu-whit, Tu-who

> Then nightly sings the staring owl –
>   Tu-who;
> Tu-whit, tu-who – a merry note,
> While greasy Joan doth keel the pot.
> Shakespeare, Love's Labor's Lost, Act V, Scene 2

For many, the sound of owls is a pleasant and merry one. Eric Hosking in his autobiography *An Eye for a Bird*, told how the nightly hooting of the pair of Tawny Owls near his home, echoing across the fields, was 'glorious music to my young

ears' and it 'lured me as surely as the Pied Piper of Hamelin.'
It can be a sound redolent of the unspoilt countryside, a
nostalgic reminder of peaceful rural ways.

For others, the sounds issuing from derelict buildings, ivy-
covered ruins, church towers, and belfries are somewhat
sinister. The Reverend Gilbert White (1720–93) wrote of the
Barn Owl (*Tyto alba*) that 'white owls often scream horribly
as they fly along: from this screaming probably arose the common people's imaginary species of Screech Owl which they
superstitiously think attends the windows of the dying.' The
same superstition is reflected in a ballad:

> Hark! Now everything is still
> The screech owl and the whistle shrill
> Call upon our dame aloud,
> And quickly bid her don her shroud.

The nocturnal noises of owls, their territorial claims and
mating calls were interpreted as messages of death and
summonses to judgement. Gilbert White curiously noted that
'most owls seem to hoot mostly in B flat.'

Far from merry was the owl in *An Elegy Written in a
Country Churchyard* by Thomas Gray (1716–71): 'The
moping owl does to the moon complain.' And sad also is
the psalmist's image of the owl:

> Because of my loud groaning
>   my bones cling to my skin.
> I am like an owl of the wilderness,
>   like a little owl of the waste places.

Psalm 102:5–6

The Silent Owl

Owls benefit from virtually silent flight: their large wings enable them to glide easily without flapping and also have a special feature – the leading edge of the foremost flight feathers are serrated and therefore break up the sound of flight by letting the air flow through them. Gilbert White observed in his *Natural History of Selborne* (1789) that 'owls move in buoyant manner, as if lighter than air. They seem to want ballast.' This allows them to come silently upon their unsuspecting prey.

In the medieval monasteries the owl became a symbol of piety because of its habit of staying quite still in a tree all through a day. This, for the monks, became a sign of meditation, the willingness to stay quiet in the presence of God in contemplation. Owls in fact remain inactive for long periods because they are digesting their prey of small mammals, often swallowed whole, head first, and requiring a lot of steady digestive-juice action.

To Attract and to Repel

Medieval parish church woodcarvers depicted an owl being mobbed by a small bird – a not uncommon event during daytime. This led to bird-hunters using an Eagle Owl (*Bubo bubo*) as a decoy on a sticky perch to lure birds to attack it. When they did, they were immobilized and caught. In the Palais des Papes in Avignon, dating from 1343, in the *Chambre des Cerfs* (the Room of the Deer), there is a painting of an owl being used as a visual decoy, with a man nearby using a whistle as an aural decoy. A similar technique to attract birds was used in Italy, while in Germany the owl was placed on the outside of a portable hide, looking like a haystack, and the lured birds were then caught with a cleft stick.

A lifelike plastic owl perches on the roof of a school in Texas to repel rather than to attract. It stands at the school's entrance to ward off unwelcome and messy visits from the pigeons of Dallas.

> A wise old owl lived in an oak.
> The more he heard the less he spoke;
> The less he spoke the more he heard,
> Why aren't we all like that old bird?
>
> A nursery rhyme

> Sweet Suffolk owl, so trimly dight,[1]
> With feathers like a lady bright,
> Thou singest alone, sitting by night,
>   Te whit, te whoo, te whit, to whit.
> Thy note, that forth so freely rolls,
> With shrill command the mouse controls,
> And sings a dirge for dying souls,
>   Te whit, te whoo, te whit, to whit.
>
> Anonymous

[1] Adorned.

10

The Peacock

Despite its high status, the domestic peacock – or, to use its more correct generic name *peafowl* (one of the prolific order Galliformes, which includes chickens) – is completely dependent on human protection. It lives for most of the year in small family groups – one male to three to five females and assorted young. It is a docile bird, good-tempered to humans and to other birds, with few needs, thriving on a diet mainly of grain and greenery. They perch on walls and roost in trees; the long train, which is made out of the well-formed outer tail feathers, is supported by the tough, stubby brown feathers of the tail itself; it is light in weight and no hindrance to flight or running fast. Cross-breeding the Indian Peafowl with the Burmese Green variety has produced a wide range of plumage colors, including the albino or white of captive birds.

As a domestic bird, the peacock's one considerable drawback – apart from its habit of eating the flowers – is its voice. The plaintive wailing cry, phonetically summarized by *paon*, the French word for peacock, sounds an alien and ghostly note in the countryside of the Western world – particularly at night. The Reverend Gilbert White, listening unwillingly to his neighbors' peacocks, commented, 'like most of the gaudy birds, his notes are grating and shocking to the ear: the yelling of cats, and the braying of an ass, are not more disgustful.'

White observed that birds are not usually blessed with a melodious voice as well as beautiful plumage. The little yellow canary is a rare exception, but on the whole the best songsters are quite drab-looking, as in the case of the nightingale. In fact, color and song both serve the same purpose – attracting a mate and making claim to a breeding or feeding ground. Obviously the peacock relies on beauty.

Across the world the pheasant family contains several rivals in the bird beauty stakes, more particularly the Chinese Golden Pheasant and the Himalayan Monal Pheasant, spectacular specimens in feather and color, designed to stand out against a background of deep jungle gloom and amid the brilliance of tropical flowers. But when the male and female of a species have highly contrasting plumage, it is usual for the male to be the more highly colored. The pea-cock typically flaunts his 'angels' feathers bright,' while his soberly dressed partner, the pea-hen, can inconspicuously lay her eggs and hatch them without arousing attention. Perhaps this marked difference in appearance is why we tend to ignore the pea-hen and commonly call the whole species 'peacocks.'

The Common Blue, or Indian, Peacock (*Pavo cristatus*) traveled from its native India through Persia (the famous Peacock Throne bears witness) via Alexander the Great to Greece and thence to Rome and, eventually, the rest of Europe. Everywhere it was admired for its ornamental beauty, trailing legends in its wake. Peacocks were brought to Palestine, too, among other precious cargo, to embellish the glories of King Solomon's reign. The biblical record reveals that Solomon had a fleet of trading ships which returned 'once in three years . . . bringing gold, and silver, ivory, and apes, and peacocks' (1 Kings 10:22).

The Peacock in Athens

Alexander the Great, during his invasion of India, was so enchanted by the sight of peacocks glittering in the dense jungles that he gave orders that none of them should be killed, and dispatched numbers of the birds back to Greece. Here it was considered at first a rare and sacred bird. It was reported how in Athens 'men of taste' paid to see the bird, and that a pair of peacocks cost several hundreds of pounds to buy.

The Beauty of the Peacock

Remember that the most beautiful things in the world are the most useless; peacocks and lilies for instance.

Stones of Venice by John Ruskin (1819–1900)

He has made everything beautiful in his time. He has also set eternity in the hearts of men; yet they cannot fathom what God has done from beginning to end.

Ecclesiastes 3:11

An authority higher and more ancient than Ruskin reminds us 'to consider the lilies' – and we might add peacocks too. The peacock figures among the most beautiful of creatures, and if 'fine feathers make fine birds,' then the peacock surely warrants consideration as 'finest bird of all.' For thousands of years the beauty of those iridescent blues and greens of the male bird's sweeping train, displayed for its courtship rituals in a magnificent, erect arc of some 200 feathers, has made the peacock an object of intense admiration. Indeed, in Hindu, Buddhist, and classical myths, alongside Muslim legends, so great was the fascination exerted by this unusually brilliant bird upon the imagination of humankind that it was believed to be invested with supernatural gifts.

It is during courtship that the male displays the full glory of his train, which continues to grow until his sixth year, and which makes up two-thirds of his 7½-feet length. However many times you have seen it, the effect of its full unfolding is breathtaking. Countless writers and poets have tried to describe it. Few have done better than G. M. Hopkins:

> He shivers when he first rears it and then again at intervals and when this happens the rest blurs and the 'eyes' start forward – I have thought it looks like a tray or green basket of fresh-cut willow hurdles set all over with Paradise fruits cut through – first through a beard of golden fibre, then through wet flesh greener than greengages or purpler than grapes.
>
> Gerard Manley Hopkins (1844–89)

The display takes place on a 'lek' or courting ground. The female, for whom this display is performed in order to entice her into his sphere of influence, and to eventual mating, shows little immediate interest, but turns away to scratch at the ground. This spurs the male into renewed efforts; he executes a series of steps, which were thought to have given that stately dance of the Tudor courts, the pavan, its name. Then he 'tramples' very quickly with his feet and runs backward towards the female. At the very last moment he sweeps round and tilts the fully extended, almost concave train towards her with a glitter of feathers and a 'clatter like the swords of sword dancers,' as Gilbert White described it. Eventually, she can resist him no longer and nature takes its course. Scientists have found that the greater the number of 'eye-spots' on the male's tail, the greater his success in attracting females.

A peahen's clutch may range from 3 to 12 eggs, which take 28 days to hatch. The young are known as pea-chicks.

The Heavenly Peacock

The religious veneration of the peacock inspired men to draw it away from its natural habitat in the jungles of India and Sri Lanka, and place it under the aegis of priests in temple precincts and rulers in the well-ordered spaces of palace gardens. The Irish poet W. B. Yeats, in his poem 'The Indian upon God,' envisages a moorfowl, a lotus, a roebuck, and a peacock, all seeing divinity in terms of themselves. The peacock says:

> Who made the grass and made the worms and made my
>   feathers gay,
> He is a monstrous peacock, and He waveth all the night
> His languid tail above us, lit with myriad spots of light.
>
> W. B. Yeats (1865–1939)

Skanda, the Hindu god of war, sits astride a peacock in a sculpture at the great temple of Angkor Wat in Cambodia (built 1112–53 CE), restating the heavenly venue, but in this Hindu shrine the bird becomes a symbol of the sun's aggressive energy. This association with the sun led humans to sacrifice peacocks in times of drought, in the hope that the rain clouds would relent at the death of this fiery bird of the sun and weep down tears of repentance upon the earth. Skanda's peacock was also the destroyer of serpents, symbolizing the sun's divine supremacy over watery beings which, unlike those spiritual and celestial, belong to the earthly, the temporal, and the physical. So powerful was the belief in the peacock's creative fire that in China one glance from the bird was supposed to make a woman pregnant! Thus fertility was added to its many supernatural attributes.

In Buddhism, we find Buddha Amitabha's red throne in the shape of a peacock, representing beauty as well as the fire of the sun's powers of regeneration. The Bodhisattva, too, taught renunciation of worldly attachments under this peacock shape and developed the theme of otherworldliness. Recalling the early association with the solar system, which may have originated because its tail was in the form of a wheel, the peacock was made the emblem of the Burmese monarchy, whose divine right to rule was believed to derive from direct descent from the sun.

The classical world also placed the peacock in the heavenly realms, making it sacred to Hera, the sky goddess wife of Zeus. In their myth Zeus becomes infatuated with the nymph Io and this arouses Hera's jealousy. To trick his wife he disguises Io as a wandering white cow (the moon) but Hera is not fooled, and requests the cow from Zeus. Hera then asks her favorite servant, the giant Argus of the hundred eyes (the stars), to guard the cow. Zeus employs the cunning Hermes, messenger of the gods, to lull Argus to sleep with stories and the music of his reed pipe. Once Argus is asleep, Hermes cuts off the creature's head, but fails to capture Io. To commemorate her faithful watchman, Hera decides to decorate the tail of her peacock with the hundred eyes of Argus. Two prominent sources of the myth of Argus's death are Aeschylus's play *Prometheus Bound* (ca. 500 BCE) and Ovid's *Metamorphoses* (ca. 8 CE). According to Ovid, "[she] saved those eyes to set them among the feathers of her peacock and filled its tail with jewels bright as stars."

Another, somewhat tamer, version of the myth recasts the 'eye' markings of the peacock's tail once more as a microcosm of the night skies with its pattern of stars, confirming the bird as a natural ally and companion of Hera in her role as goddess of the skies.

Peacock in Religious Art

By the time of the Renaissance, the peacock had a secure position in Christian iconography, but not as the symbol of pride by which it is better known today. It had passed from its pagan status as Hera's bird into a reminder of the resurrection. This may have come from a belief mentioned by St. Augustine that its flesh was incorruptible, or perhaps because it sheds its tail feathers every year, to renew them more gloriously in the spring. To which the bestiaries also added their moral contribution: the peacock cries out in fear as it awakes each day, having dreamt that it has lost its beauty. The moral here being that a Christian should cry out in fear of losing those good qualities with which God has endowed his soul, and that will ensure his eternal life.

Peacocks are made to figure somewhat incongruously alongside more familiar farmyard animals in paintings of the nativity, perched on the stable roof, or beside the manger, as Tintoretto (1518–94) imagined it in his painting in the Scuola di San Rocco in Venice, a potent reminder of Jesus's death and resurrection. But at the same time it also signifies the all-seeing church (in the 'eyes' of the tail), which, on earth, will continue the work and embody the life of Christ.

The Low Countries followed suit. For example, the Flemish painter Peter Paul Rubens (1577–1640), admired and knighted by the English King Charles I, painted in 1612 his magnificent triptych in Antwerp cathedral entitled *The Descent from the Cross*. On a side panel of the Visitation, under an arch, he discreetly lodged a peacock, again indicating Jesus's future resurrection.

An unusual reflection on this theme is found in a Byzantine mosaic at Tabgah, near Capernaum. It depicts Jesus's miracle of the loaves and fishes, but the Master is accompanied by a peacock. This is an allusion to chapter 6 of John's gospel where Jesus speaks of himself as the bread of eternal life, the token presence of the peacock once again prefiguring his resurrection. It is not difficult to understand how the 'bird of the hundred eyes' thus came to be linked to the beatific vision, that state of eternal bliss when the soul comes face-to-face (eye-to-eye) with the Godhead.

The Flesh of the Peacock

The Romans acquired a taste for peacocks. According to Pliny, it was M. Aufidius Lurco, a renowned glutton, who first had them fattened for the table and then went wholesale, making a sizeable fortune supplying them to others. Peacock flesh is tough and unpalatable, so it was served more for effect than flavor. The roasted bird was brought to the table with its beak gilded and its tail feathers in a decorative fan, a dazzling semicircle of iridescence raised in exotic tribute round its rump.

Later, in England, it was served up at royal banquets in similar style, but encased in pastry ('peacock pie'). But it was quickly ousted when turkeys started being imported from Mexico in the mid-sixteenth century. 'Turkeys, heresies, hops and beer, Came into England all in one year' went a contemporary, if inaccurate, jingle. Although less easy on the eye than the peacock, turkey was definitely tastier on the tongue.

Peacock meat was in fact so tough that there arose the belief, as mentioned, that peacock flesh was indestructible, and thus the bird arrived, via another route, as a symbol of immortality. The pagan symbol was later adopted by Christianity but transformed to signify victory over death and the resurrection of the dead. 'For who except God, the Creator of all things, endowed the flesh of the dead peacock with the power of never decaying?' asked St. Augustine of Hippo. Which proves that even a great intellect like Augustine can nod if he forgoes close observation.

The Western church deepened this symbolic significance of the bird by depicting it drinking from the eucharistic chalice, showing how creation shared with humanity in Christ's eternal redemption. In the Eastern church it is sometimes seen on either side of the Tree of Life, demonstrating the incorruptibility of the human soul and the twofold nature of humankind's psyche, the spiritual and the carnal.

Peacock as Code Word

The peacock's singular beauty inspired humans far and wide, no more so than in that mystical element of Islam called Sufism. Devout contemplatives are found in all religions who seek to find union with God by denying themselves and abandoning most human distractions and affections in order to meditate on the Godhead alone. By this course of prayer, meditation and ascetic practice, their soul, the divine element in them, is released into sharing the very life of God himself, while his worshippers remain earthbound. To describe their journeys and visions strains both language and perception to their limits, inspiring a new, rich vocabulary of symbol and metaphor. But at the same time, Sufis wished to guard against fraudulent use of their hard-earned spiritual labors by those without the understanding and experience to make wise use of them. To avoid this, they devised codes known only to the initiated.

The peacock and its magnificent spread tail provided the Sufis with a powerful image of how God links humankind to himself. They pictured God's Spirit as a peacock looking at itself, with its hundred eyes, in the mirror of the Divine Essence. So fervently in awe of its reflected glory was it, that drops of its sweat fell to the ground: those drops become all created things. In other words, the Godhead, contemplating himself, is compelled by his love to reproduce himself, which he does by his creation of all living things. Likewise man, meditating upon God, will produce the fruits of God's Spirit, those states and acts of love that reflect the very nature of God.

Peacock symbols abound in the Sufis' artistic and poetic expression, no more so than in those encoded in the Mughal paintings of the royal gardens of the sixteenth century. But there is more here than first meets the eye. Their word for peacock, *tauus*, also means 'verdant land,' the Sufi code word for meditation/contemplation, the quest of the soul for its paradise or divine home. Thus the garden court of the Mughal emperor could be seen as that heavenly paradise whose image is the peacock.

The Peacock's Cry

There are many legends explaining why the peacock makes his barbaric cry. One ancient and popular understanding was that it is always bewailing its ugly feet. In 1258 the Persian poet Sa'id wrote that while others are praising its rich and variegated plumage, the peacock himself is blushing at the sight of his ugly feet. They are in fact larger but no uglier than those of other birds. Some said that its cry was a lament at the fear of losing its beauty, and that its beauty was also its constant burden. While to others it was a timely, if too constant, reminder of the Christian soul crying out to God.

W. B. Yeats adds a somewhat macabre twist to the last interpretation. He was outlining the tragic collapse of human values in the world in his prose piece 'The Vision,' and could find no better image with which to describe the last gasp of civilization than that of the peacock's despairing cry:

> A civilization is a struggle to keep self-control, and in this is like some great tragic person, some Niobe, who must display an almost superhuman will or the cry will not touch our sympathy. The loss of control over thought comes towards the end; first a sinking in upon the moral being, the last surrender, the irrational cry, revelation – the scream of Juno's peacock.
>
> W. B. Yeats (1865–1939)

'Like Niobe all tears' is how Shakespeare referred to the legend of Queen Niobe who lost all her children when she vaunted their virtues above the children of the goddess Leto.

Leto's children, Artemis and Apollo, proceeded to slay the queen's children and then, later, slew her, but not until after she had frantically cried out her grief.

A more prosaic piece of folklore was that the peacocks cried out when rain was on the way – perhaps at the thought of all those long feathers getting wet. Robert Chester hedged his bets by offering two of these explanations in his poem 'Love's Martyr':

> The proud sun-loving peacock with his feathers
> Walks alone, thinking himself a king;
> And with his voice prognosticates all weathers
> Although God knows but badly doth he sing.
> But when he looks down to his base black feet,
> He droops, and is ashamed of things unmete.
>
> *Love's Martyr* (1601) by Robert Chester

Peacocks in Private Collections

Percy Bysshe Shelley (1792–1822), writing to his friend and fellow author, coincidentally called Thomas Love Peacock, in August 1821, describes to him Lord Byron's palace home in Ravenna:

> Lord B's establishment consists, besides servants, of ten horses, eight enormous dogs, three monkeys, five cats, an eagle, a crow, and a falcon; and all of these, except the horses, walk about the house, which every now and then resounds to their unarbitrated quarrels, as if they were masters of it.

He then adds a PS:

> After I have sealed my letter, I find that my enumeration of the animals in this Circean Palace was defective, and that in

a material point. I have just met on the grand staircase five peacocks, three guinea hens, and an Egyptian crane.

Dante Gabriel Rossetti (1828–82), one of the Pre-Raphaelite group of artists in nineteenth-century England, also entertained some odd houseguests at his Chelsea home in London. Some of the more exotic inmates of his menagerie were a wombat, a white bull, a racoon, a kangaroo, and, lastly, a white peacock. Distracted from their care by too many cares of his own, Rossetti neglected his poor creatures. One day a visitor, by chance looking under the sofa, found the latest victim of that neglect, the poor white peacock – bedraggled and quite dead.

Rossetti later joined ranks with William Morris, the great champion of craftsmanship, who himself wove a magnificent green peacock into his famous tapestry, 'The Forest.'

The Pride of the Peacock

The sumptuous effect of 'the peacock in his pride' with tail outspread was copied in precious stones for the thrones of the Mughal emperors in Persia and India. The 'peacock throne' became a byword for all that was lavish and luxurious. However, this 'pride' of the peacock was also judged from earliest times to be a different, less commendable sort of pride, the first and chief of the Seven Deadly Sins, personal vanity and an undue obsession with appearances. 'Proud as a peacock' was a common phrase from the fourteenth century and no doubt found fresh emphasis in a later age from those strutting birds in the parklands of stately homes. The bird's very demeanor appears to be haughty, while its gait is sedate and measured with head often held high or bobbing as though in acknowledgement of adulation. Always quick to discover failings in others, we are only too willing to suspect in beauty the worst of morals. (Incidentally, the 'bobbing' motion of the peacock's head is to allow it to stabilize its focus, so that it can pick out its food.)

This prideful aspect came to a somewhat odd but notorious prominence in the nineteenth century by the public airing of a quarrel between James McNeill Whistler and the shipping magnate and nouveau riche Frederick R. Leyland. The latter wanted to become a modern Medici, a patron of the arts, and had bought many paintings for his new home in London, among them a Whistler, this last to adorn the dining room. Somehow Whistler became involved in the redecoration of the whole room, which mushroomed wildly into an utterly out-landish extravaganza, celebrated by Whistler as his 'Peacock Room.' He lavished peacocks on walls, ceiling, and shutters and, in ecstatic mode, gilded every molding and projection with golds and blues, like the exterior of some lacquered box. He even painted over invaluable antique leather wall cover-ing. It was definitely de trop both in design and execution and, above all, in cost. Leyland objected and, initially, refused any payment; the press were invited in and publicity, much adverse, duly circulated. For Whistler, as for so many others, pride went before a fall; he was virtually bankrupted.

The peacock was also regarded darkly in the superstition that the 'eyes' in its train are in fact an emblem of the Evil Eye, and of all acts of betrayal or treachery. For some, the eye feathers became objects of fear, not admiration, and shunned as tokens of misfortune and liable to bring disaster on their owner. No girl dared to keep a peacock's feather in her bed-room: it was considered a certain way of making her stay single for the rest of her life.

An old legend explained these superstitions: when God created the first peacock, the Seven Deadly Sins were envious of its beauty. God punished them by taking away the colors by which they were identified – for example, the green eye of Envy and the red eye of Anger, and set them in the feathers of the peacock. Ever since, the Sins have dogged the trail of the peacock, trying to seize an opportunity to get back their eyes.

William Blake (1757–1827) rebutted all slanders against the bird when he wrote, 'The pride of the peacock is the glory of God.' The peacock's beauty is a part of the eternal qualities of Truth, Beauty, and Goodness. The peacock stands proudly in vindication of beauty and all that beauty brings to our lives.

11

The Pelican

The United States and Europe have roughly one third of their bird populations in common, with another third related to each other. The remaining third are exclusive to each continent, including such well-known birds as the Cardinal and Bluebird in America and the Nightingale in Europe. Pelicans occupy the common middle ground together with other members of their order, like the Shag, Cormorant, and Gannet. The order has the singular feature of being totipalmate, that is having webbing across all four toes, whereas in all other waders or seabirds, the webbing covers only three toes. The result is creatures of great swimming prowess. The pelican family itself (Pelecanidae) has the additional peculiar feature of having one vertebra in its neck without a hinge so that it cannot lift its neck. But the pelican's most unique feature is its huge throat pouch, a membranous distensible bag suspended from the lower mandible of its

very large bill. It uses the pouch like a solid net, scooping up 2 to 3 gallons of water that – with its catch of fish – can weigh up to 24 pounds. It then squeezes the water out before taking flight to the feeding site where it will regurgitate its contents for its young. The old Hebrew word for the bird was *q'aat*, meaning 'vomiter,' and we can see why. Perhaps that is also why it was numbered among those birds in Leviticus called 'abominations.'

The American White Pelican (*Pelecanus erythrorhynchos*, 'pelican with a red bill') fishes on the surface of freshwater in organized flotillas. Flocks work together in horseshoe formation to drive the fish into shallower water before scooping them up. The Brown Pelican (*Pelecanus occidentalis*, 'eastern pelican') by contrast dives spectacularly into the sea from a height of some 60 feet or more for its catch. It lives strictly along the coasts, but sometimes strays inland.

Although the White Pelican stands some four feet tall with a wingspan of eight to nine feet and can weigh over twenty pounds, its poundage is in its feathers! A pelican's bones account for only one and a half pounds of the total – they are hollows filled with air. (A thirteenth-century treatise for anchoresses, *Ancrene Wisse*, described pelicans as of 'little flesh and many feathers.') Without these airy bones, the brown species would find it hard to resurface after a dive; it rises easily because the contained air propels it upwards through the water.

Once airborne, a difficult feat in itself, both pelicans are consummate fliers, traveling in skeins at considerable heights over long distances, and making daily journeys of upwards of 100 miles from nesting sites to feeding grounds. Pelicans also travel far in their migrations, summering in much of the northern United States and in parts of Canada. A delighted observer of this phenomenon in 1872 was the French Impressionist painter Edgar Degas who, as he approached New York on board the *SS Scotia*, covered three pages of his sketchbook with images of the white pelicans he saw in the harbor approaches.

In the mating season the white species alone sports a bright orange, stand-up fibrous plate on the upper mandible of its bill; the plate is discarded as the season ends (as is the Puffin's multi-colored bill). It also grows a yellow crest as part of its courting apparel. Both species are colonial nesters, congregating in great numbers, the white on the ground on islands, with the brown preferring to perch and build on trees. Eggs are incubated on or under foot, and once hatched the young are precocial (active on birth). Later they are kept protected in a crèche by one or two adult birds, but still fed individually by the parents; a similar upbringing is found only among flamingos, eider ducks, and penguins.

Pelican Alert

The stately, white procession of pelicans at a great height in full flight with their slow, measured wing flap and glide momentum is one of those passages of nature which seem to signal a permanence that cannot be shaken.

This too was the vision of John Audubon when – on his travels through the American wilderness in 1838 – he first discovered the white pelican. He was so impressed by its majestic presence in the air and on water that thinking (wrongly as it happened) it was uniquely indigenous, he named it *Americanus*. He wrote, 'In consequence of this discovery, I have honoured it with the name of my beloved country, over the mighty streams of which may this splendid bird wander free and unmolested to the most distant times, as it has already done down the misty ages of unknown antiquity.'

It was a strangely prescient wish. For 50 years later, man's greed in the form of the 'plume trade' (feathers for hats and costumes) threatened the bird's very existence. At its zenith it

cruelly and wantonly plundered whole pelican colonies, deci-
mating their populations. And then, in the mid-twentieth century, another terrible scourge was introduced, the toxic
pesticide DDT, with its devastating effects on all wildlife. If
the marine biologist Rachel Carson had not challenged the
chemical industry and our blind faith in technological
progress at the expense of nature, DDT may well have
destroyed much of America's native wildlife. Her book *Silent
Spring* (1962) alerted the public to the pesticide's terrible
effects. Carson wrote that we are 'challenged as mankind has
never been challenged before to prove our maturity and our
mastery, not of nature, but of ourselves.'

Among the most vulnerable groups of birds were the order
Pelecaniformes; pelicans are among those creatures high in the
food chain and therefore at great risk, and this was the case particularly with the Brown Pelicans of Louisiana, already reduced
by some 90 percent. Fortunately, the lobby of the environmental movement had DDT banned in 1972 and all pelican species
rebounded dramatically and are now doing well.

Pelican and Laughing Gull

Once upon a time, at the beginning of the world when everything was changing all the time, the Gull and the Pelican
looked at each other, and discovered an odd fact. The Gull
had a long bill but a short body, while the Pelican had a long
body but a short bill. They were not happy with this arrange-
ment, for the Pelican could not get enough fish to eat for his
large body with his short bill, and the Gull was hampered in
his flight by his long heavy bill. What to do?

The two birds decided to trade bills! But the cunning Gull
realized the Pelican had more to gain (in fish) from this trade,
so he set about convincing his fellow bird, who was somewhat
slow on the uptake, to share with him a portion of his fish
catch each time he made one. After much hard bargaining,

they agreed that half the Pelican's catch, on demand, would be the fairest division.

The Pelican immediately tried out his fishing skills with his new bill. Down he dived and up he came with a bill full of fish. Wonderful! As he tilted his head back to let the water drain out of his pouch, he felt a sharp stab on his head. It was the Gull who gave him a whole lot of pecks with his new small, pointed beak.

'Remember our agreement,' the Gull screamed in the Pelican's ear, 'Half! Half! Half!' – pronounced 'harf,' the English way – and the Pelican did remember. And to this day, the Gull, the one now called the Laughing Gull, who patrols the Virgin Islands, makes exactly the same, laughing cry – 'Half! Half! Half!' – and steals the Pelican's hard-won catch.

The Pious Pelican

There was a belief, of Egyptian origin according to St. Isidore (560–636), that the pelican pecked at its breast to let its young feed on its own blood. This understanding was probably due to a mistaken observation of how the bird regurgitates great quantities of fish to its young from its throat pouch. In the mating season the pouch turns a red color and can look as though it is full of blood; the young peck at it for their food delivery and so appear to be extracting blood from the parent bird. Some pelicans also grow breast feathers that are red during the time the nestlings are feeding. Without questioning its scientific truth, St. Augustine of Hippo saw a potential Christian message in this phenomenon and so transformed it into a much-revered image of Charity.

Medieval Christianity took up the theme and elaborated it, and thus the bird became a multifaceted symbol of charity and self-giving. St. Gertrude (1256–1302) – the German mystic and present-day patroness of the West Indies – had a vision of Christ as a pelican feeding humankind with his blood, which found expression in a low relief on the great bronze doors of Cologne Cathedral. Likewise in Durham Cathedral a lectern was cast in the form of a pelican, signifying Jesus Christ, the Word of God, feeding the world with the gospel; in the same cathedral before the suppression of the monasteries by Henry VIII in 1538, the sacrament was reserved in a tabernacle in the shape of a silver pelican and suspended above the high altar.

Because the pelican brought life out of death, the connection with the resurrection was made, and it became commonplace in the Middle Ages for artists to portray this by placing pelicans on their nest above Christ's Cross. Dante was so inspired by this resurrection motif that he called Jesus Christ *nostro pelicano*.

The medieval moralizing treatise *Bestiarum* ('Of the Beasts') in the Royal Library in Brussels contains the macabre innovation that the young birds were killed by their father for their cruelty to him, but were then restored to life by the mother for pity's sake. Another version, which St. Jerome (342–420) followed, has the story of the young ones being destroyed by serpents, so illustrating the destruction of humankind by the Old Serpent, Satan, and restored to life by the salvation of the blood of Christ.

Later, Guillaume du Bartas (1544–90), French soldier and poet of the epic *La Semaine* ('The Week' [of Creation]), summarizes the story in these fine verses from a contemporaneous translation by Joshua Sylvester:

> The Pelican kindly, for her tender brood,
> Tears her own bowels, trilleth out her blood
> To heal her young; and in a wondrous sort
> Unto her children doth her life disport.
> A type of Christ, who, sin-thralled man to free,
> Became a captive, and on a shameful Tree
> Self-guiltless shed his blood, by's wounds to save us,
> And heal the wounds th'old serpent gave us.

And so became of mere immortal mortal,
Thereby to make frail mortal immortal.

The English poet laureate John Skelton (1460?–1529) abbreviates it *con brio* in these six terse lines from his 'Armonye of Birds':

> Then sayd the Pellycane,
> When my byrdes be slayne
> With my blood I them revive.
> Scripture doth record
> The same dyd for our Lord
> And rose from deth to lyve.

The bird's natural migration habits added yet another allegorical layer to this image, for in the summer the bird disappeared with the sun, but reappeared in winter with the life-giving rains. This reminded the faithful of the salvation teaching found in the gospel accounts of the passion, in which Jesus's side is pierced and from which streamed both water and the blood.

Freemasonry, too, was to use the pelican motif to enjoin its members to the discipline of self-sacrifice, combining the reference to the Temple gushing water mentioned in Ezekiel 47 with the pelican's renowned charity.

The mystics as well were inspired by the image of life-giving water and blood; Johannes Scheffler, better known as Angelus Silesius (1624–77), wrote, 'Behold, our Pelican waters you with his blood and the waters of his heart. If you accept them fittingly . . . you will at once be alive and well.'

The Reformation retained the symbol, which matured in William Shakespeare's imagination, as in the following lines from *Hamlet*:

> To his good friends thus wide I'll ope my arms,
> And, like the kind, life-rendering pelican,
> Refresh them with my blood.

The image was so enduring that even the bawdy comedy of manners of Restoration drama found a place for it, as in William Congreve's *Love for Love* (1695): 'What, would'st thou have me turn pelican, and feed thee on my own vitals?'

But for the Romantics the image was turned inwards to become synonymous with the poet's own life and destiny. Alfred de Musset (1810–57) in his 'Nuit de Mai' ('Night of May') pictures the pelican returning exhausted from a long journey. He has found nothing with which to assuage his children's hunger, so he gives them his own heart. Then, when at death's door, he realizes his fatal predicament, and narrowly escapes from them with a last dreadful cry of 'adieu.' De Musset writes: 'Poète, c'est ainsi que font les grands poètes' ('It is thus that great poets act').

The image underwent another transformation in Edith Wharton's short story 'The Pelican,' in which the perverse mother Mrs. Amyat pretends she is sacrificing her all for her son 'the baby,' when in fact it is all done for her own twisted ends.

Pelican Rock

In 1775, a ship slowly edges its way through the fog that fills the great bay on the coast of California and reduces visibility to a few yards, muffling the sounds of the sea. Suddenly the navigator is startled by a strange noise in front of him; it is the rapid clattering of massive wings as a flock of pelicans explodes from beneath the very bows of the ship. At that same moment a gigantic rock looms immediately ahead, and only by violently swinging the wheel does he avert shipwreck. He says a quick prayer of thanksgiving beneath his breath and watches as the cliff slips safely by the tilting decks.

Thus the Spanish explorer Juan Manuel de Ayala, as he charted the great sweep of the bay of San Francisco, discovered that dangerous rock and, on behalf of his avian deliverers, named it *La Isla de los Alcatraces* ('The Island of the Pelicans'). Many years later the name was shortened to 'Alcatraz,' or just 'The Rock,' the most notorious prison in the United States.

Perhaps its best-known prisoner was 'The Birdman,' Robert F. Stroud, made famous in the film 'The Birdman of Alcatraz' in which Burt Lancaster has the starring role. Stroud in fact did not keep birds at Alcatraz but at Leavenworth Federal Penitentiary in Kansas, where he became such an expert in the breeding and diseases of canaries that he was given an extra cell in which to contain all his scientific research and his birds. He also published learned books on the subject. But, contrary to the gentrified portrayal of him by Lancaster, and despite his high IQ, he was a violent prisoner, who had once killed a prison guard and had to be transferred to Alcatraz in 1942 after showing threatening behavior to other inmates. He remained in solitary confinement on the Rock for the rest of his life, dying in 1963.

Alcatraz today is on the tourist trail, but its earliest inmates have returned in numbers. It is now home to seabirds once more, with over 900 breeding pairs of Western Gulls, as well as the Black-crowned Night Heron, and Brandt's Cormorant. Alas, no pelicans are to be seen – at least not yet.

On the Atlantic coast of the United States another pelican was linked to a near disaster some two hundred years before. In 1577 Sir Francis Drake embarked from Plymouth in England on his circumnavigation of the globe with five ships, commanding his own 100-tonner, 'The Pelican.' After weeks of foul weather and the disclosure of the projected extent of the journey, Drake's sailors mutinied. Having executed the ringleader, his friend Thomas Doughty, Drake got rid of two of the ships and, possibly out of superstition, renamed his own 'The Golden Hind.' He was to return four years later to fame and in possession of an immense fortune, but the name of 'The Pelican' was forgotten.

The Heraldic Pelican

In heraldry it is the mystic charitable aspect of the pelican that is always portrayed as she sustains her children with her own blood. The heraldic term for this is 'a pelican in her piety' and has the mother bird on a nest with her young beneath or beside her. However, when shown without the children, the theme is continued and she is described as 'vulning herself' (from the Latin *vulnare*, 'to wound'). The actual portrayal of the bird often bears small resemblance to a pelican, but is nearer in appearance to an eagle, with sharp curved beak and shorter rounded feathers.

In the thirteenth century Pope Urban IV instituted the Feast of Corpus Christi to celebrate the institution and gift of the Eucharist. This followed on a vision given to Blessed Juliana, the devout nun of Liège, in 1230. The feast day entered the church calendar on the Thursday after Trinity Sunday. The pope commanded its observance in the bull *Transiturus*. To give the feast its greatest impact, he asked the learned Dominican St. Thomas Aquinas to write two hymns for it. In the hymn of thanksgiving *Adoro Te Devote*, we find the following lines:

> Pelican of mercy, Jesu, Lord and God,
> Cleanse me wretched sinner, in thy precious Blood;
> Blood whereof one drop for humankind outpoured,
> Might from all transgressions have the world restored.

Both Oxford and Cambridge universities have colleges called Corpus Christi. Cambridge's was founded in 1351 by the two Guilds of Corpus Christi and The Blessed Virgin, while Oxford's later foundation dates from 1517 and the good offices of Richard Foxe, bishop of Winchester. And both have coats of arms containing the pelican – Cambridge choosing the pelican in its piety and Oxford the solitary bird, which is also seen in its main quad on a sundial built in 1551. A link to the United States was made when Sir William Mather, a Manchester industrialist and member of Parliament donated an exact replica of this sundial to Princeton University in 1907. It still stands in the quad before McCosh Hall and its 20-foot height is identically crowned with a pelican vulning itself.

Pelican Words

The word pelican comes to us directly from the Greek *pelikus*, meaning an axe, which itself is closely linked to the Greek for 'woodpecker.' The axe in question, resembling the beak of either bird, is more likely to be a slim adze than a hatchet with its square face. The indigenous people of New Caledonia use a 'pelican's head,' a round-headed, wooden war club with a projecting beak of iron.

Another sort of weapon, another sort of war: at one time our ancestors were faced with a horrendous dental extraction implement called 'a pelican,' a very nasty instrument with a long curved 'beak.' Surely the modern dental drill pales into insignificance beside this weapon of torture!

For some obscure reason, a piece of ancient ordnance was given the name pelican. It was a cannon or culverin, carrying a shot of six pounds weight, and the name was interchangeable with the cannonball itself. In 1754, on October 6, Horace Walpole wrote in a letter, 'When your relation, General Guise, was marching up to Carthegena, and the pelicans whistled round him, he said, "What would Chloe [the duke of Newcastle's cook] give for these to make a pelican pie?"' It was to the dense round balls of suet used in stews that he probably referred. Pelicans do appear in ancient cookbooks, but are not highly commended, what little meat the carcase yields up being tough in the extreme.

But asking for a 'pelican' can get you more than bad stew. If you go into a bar in parts of the country and order a 'brown pelican' you will not be served the bird but a variation of the English 'shandy,' a drink of half beer and half lemonade or ginger beer. This brown concoction is made with apple cider and beer, loaded with ice and served in a highball glass.

The Pelican's Friends

A father and son, German immigrants called Kroegel, in 1881 trekked overland from Ohio to Sebastian in Florida where they set up home on the west bank of the Indian River Lagoon. Across the water they were in full view of a six-acre island, a nesting place for thousands of Brown Pelicans and aptly named Pelican Island. Despite leading busy and successful lives, the two took a protective interest in the birds, especially when their existence was threatened by feather bounty hunters.

After years of fighting for the birds' survival in what was becoming one of their last breeding grounds on the East Coast, the Kroegels received much needed support in the person of Frank Chapman of the American Museum of Natural History in New York, and from the Florida Audubon Society. A joint appeal was sent to President Theodore Roosevelt, with the result that a presidential order was signed in March 1903, designating Pelican Island as the first National Wildlife Refuge, land set aside for the sole purpose of wildlife conservation. So began the National Wildlife Refuge System of the United States with its national parks and conservation enforcement laws.

The Solitary Pelican

Pelicans sitting alone on land digesting their catch of fish present a sight to the human eye of utter dejection; their heads and bills tucked down to their breasts and a mournful look in their eye. This is taken up by the psalmist when he writes in Psalm 102, 'I am like a pelican of the wilderness.' By the use of this incongruous image he gives us a sense of his rejection by society and consequent abandonment, alone, in a desolate place. In a similar fashion, both Isaiah (34:11) and Zephaniah (2:14) likened the utter desolation of the nations to a pelican dwelling in desert places. The early church read this as a type of Christ's own destiny, both in his temptations in the wilderness at the beginning of his ministry and in the story of his passion.

In the twelfth-century *Aberdeen Bestiary* we can see how the medieval understanding had elaborated this image. Here the 'Bird of Egypt' (the pelican), living in the wilderness of the Nile, has become Jesus Christ made solitary because he is the only person ever born of a virgin. His solitary state signifies his freedom from sin as evident in his life; the wilderness that state which is free from the harmful preoccupations of the world.

Thomas Traherne (1637–74), the metaphysical poet, wrote 'a man that Studies Happiness must sit alone like a sparrow upon the House Top, and like a Pelican in the Wilderness,' introducing the thought that without an inner unity which is independent of external supports, there can be no contentment.

Memorial Pelican

At the eastern end of St. Paul's Cathedral in London, behind the high altar, is the beautiful American Memorial Chapel, commemorating those American servicemen who had been based in Britain and had lost their lives in World War II. In front of the chapel, which was dedicated in 1958, there is a Roll of Honor containing the names of 28,000 servicemen, written by hand on vellum. A Bald Eagle is on the cover of this volume of remembrance. The chapel has three stained-glass windows; one of them carries the Brown Pelican of Louisiana.

(The state seal of Louisiana is a pelican in its piety surrounded by the motto, 'Union, Justice, Confidence.') Below the windows are oak and limewood carvings of birds, plants, and animals native to America; they include the Scrub Jay, the Scarlet Tanager, the Quail, the Osprey, and the Bobolink.

12

The Raven

Tweedledum and Tweedledee
Agreed to have a battle;
For Tweedledum said Tweedledee
Had spoiled his nice new rattle.

Just then flew down a monstrous crow,
As black as a tar-barrel;
Which frightened both the heroes so,
They quite forgot their quarrel.

Through the Looking Glass by Lewis Carroll (1832–98)

For thousands of years people have been frightened by that 'monstrous crow,' the raven. *Corvus corax* is the biggest of the corvids or crow family, noted for their dark plumage, powerful bills, intelligence, and aggressive behavior; theirs is a family that includes magpies, jays, and rooks. In the Northern Hemisphere, especially in northern Europe, the raven is one of the most powerful birds of Norse mythology. Odin, the god of war, had two raven spies called Hugin and Munin, whose names can be roughly translated as 'Thought' and 'Memory.' Each morning Odin sent them off to fly round the world to learn what was going on and when at dusk they returned to perch one on each shoulder, the birds croaked in their master's ears the news of the day. Odin himself was known as the *Hrafngud* or 'Raven God.'

The Danes marched into battle under a standard decorated with a huge raven. It was said that when victory was in sight, the flag streamed out bravely and the raven stood up with pride, but when defeat beckoned, both flag and raven drooped. Vikings raiding from the Baltic North filled the inhabitants of northern Britain with fear as their longboats were sighted with the fearsome black raven fluttering at the masthead. The folk memory remained long after the Vikings were dead and gone; even in the nineteenth century York-shire parents would frighten badly behaved children by saying, 'the raven will get you,' instead of the more usual 'bogeyman.'

It is not surprising that this huge bird – two feet long and black from head to tail – sent shivers down the spines of our ancestors. Even if its hoarse croak, beady black eye, and bouncy sideways gait were not sinister enough, it was also associated with war and death by its scavenging presence on the battlefield. As a carrion-eater of high intelligence, the raven learnt that the assembly of armies predicted human slaughter, and so it became a camp follower of those armies and the most dedicated scavenger of the rich human pickings from those killing fields.

The Ravenous Bird

It was not only the war dead that provided the raven with its next meal. In Neolithic times it was the custom to lay the dead out before burial; the raven, and its smaller relative the carrion crow, then picked the bones clean, just as vultures are still allowed to do in parts of India. The raven added to its macabre reputation by its habit of first pecking out the eyes of the corpse. In an old Scottish ballad, 'The Twa Corbies,' the two ravens of the title are overheard making plans to 'dine' on a 'new-slain knight': 'I'll pike out his bonny blue e'en [eyes],' says one. It has been suggested that ravens attack the eyes first to make sure their dinner is quite dead – or to finish it off, if it is not!

It is not for nothing that we have the word 'ravenous' in our vocabulary, for the raven is an omnivore of astonishing variety. In sheep country, ravens help to dispose of dead lambs and, given the opportunity, they dispatch live ones, too. They also follow wolf packs and clear up whatever remains after a kill, enjoying an unusually tolerant relationship with these fierce hunters. But apart from carrion, ravens satisfy their appetites with a whole range of food, including small birds and animals that they catch and kill, birds' eggs, seeds, and a host of other items.

The Prophetic Raven

As the raven was seen so often around the dead and dying, it was a small step for superstitious people to believe that it could prophesy death, and that its very presence foretold the event: 'The raven himself is hoarse that croaks the fatal entrance of Duncan under my battlements,' states Lady Macbeth in Shakespeare's play, as proof that her husband is destined to murder the king.

Another play written in the sixteenth century, *The Jew of Malta* by Christopher Marlowe, also has a raven spreading doom and gloom:

> The sad presaging raven, that tolls
> The sick man's passport in her hollow beak
> And in the shadow of the silent night
> Doth shake contagion from her sable wing.
>
> Christopher Marlowe (1564–93)

This prophetic role assigned the raven was part of Roman lore, too. The brilliant orator, lawyer, and politician Cicero was supposed to have been warned of his death by the fluttering and flapping of ravens about his ship as he fled from Caesar. And, according to the Roman historian Plutarch, the birds later flew into Cicero's bedroom on the day he was to be murdered, plucked at the bedclothes and croaked their doomladen message.

In Ireland the old expression 'ravens' knowledge' signified 'to see and understand everything.' Ravens are undoubtedly very intelligent – tests have shown that they can count up to eight and learn to mimic words – but perhaps the Hebridean meaning of the saying is nearer the truth: there 'ravens' knowledge' meant 'knowing the whereabouts of a dead body.'

The Benign Raven

The raven has also been considered as benign, benevolent, and beneficial. Native American peoples of the Pacific Northwest once considered the raven as the god who brought life and order to earth, a divine thief who stole the light from the power who wanted to keep the world in darkness.

In folk medicine, as well, ravens were believed to cure bad eyesight and exercise the power to restore sight to the blind. Belief in their healing gifts probably derives from an association of ideas: ravens had been observed destroying eyes; therefore, it was argued, they must be capable of restoring them!

Although considered unclean to eat because of their own carrion tastes, ravens in the Bible have a generally good reputation and enjoy the distinction of being the first bird to be mentioned by name:

> And it came to pass at the end of forty days, that Noah opened the window of the ark which he had made and he sent forth a raven, which went forth to and fro, until the waters were dried up from off the earth.

> Genesis 8:6–7

Noah, who was well placed on his floating conservation center to study the natural habits of birds, would have chosen his aerial spy quite consciously, for the raven is a strong flier, with great stamina, who can cover long distances; and in this instance, we can suppose that Noah's raven easily fed himself on the floating corpses of the flood waters.

Later on in the Bible, it is ravens who provide a prophet's food: when Elijah 'went and did according unto the word of the Lord . . . and dwelt by the brook Cherith, that is before Jordan,' ravens 'brought him bread and flesh in the morning, and bread and flesh in the evening' (1 Kings 17:5–6). One theory ventures that it was not ravens at all, but rather people who carried out this mercy mission. A mistake in transcription could have substituted *orab*, Hebrew for 'raven,' for *orabim*, the inhabitants of the village of Orab. But the story of the black birds flying in heavenly provender is much more imaginative and reflects well on the ravens!

Perhaps it was the Elijah story that gave rise to several similar accounts of ravens supplying beneficient services to the saints as avian quartermasters or by standing sentry. In his life of the first Christian hermit, St. Paul the Hermit (died ca. 345 CE), St. Jerome describes a desert meeting between the then centenarian hermit and the founder of Christian monasticism, St. Antony of Egypt (251–356 CE). In Jerome's account it was a raven who supplied the saints with the bread for their shared meal. And again, according to tradition, it was a raven, too, who stood sentinel over the body of the martyred fourth-century St. Vincent of Saragossa. The rock where the saint is buried is called 'Raven's Rock' and the church that was built there is called 'the Church of the Ravens.'

The Playful Raven

Ravens are extremely acrobatic aeronauts. They look as though they are thoroughly enjoying themselves as they twist and tumble and nose-dive in the air. Gilbert White observed:

> There is a peculiarity belonging to ravens that must draw the attention even of the most incurious – they spend all their leisure time in striking and cuffing each other on the wing in a kind of playful skirmish; and, when they move from one place to another, frequently turn on their backs with a loud croak, and seem to be falling to the ground. . . .
>
> Gilbert White (1720–93)

Literary Ravens

Two famous literary ravens are 'Grip,' who goes everywhere, even into prison, with his poor simple master, Barnaby Rudge, in Charles Dickens's book of that name, and the 'grim, ghastly, gaunt, and ominous bird of yore,' in Edgar Allan Poe's poem 'The Raven,' first published in New York in 1845.

It appears that there is a transatlantic connection between these two birds. The poet's bird of doom was originally intended to be an owl, but the American – having just reviewed Dickens's book – changed his bird to a raven. The two, though linked, were not similarly gifted. Dickens's 'Grip' had quite a large vocabulary, including 'I'm a devil,' 'Never say die,' and, after much effort, the whole of the nursery rhyme 'Polly put the kettle on.' Its American counterpart could only manage one word, which it keeps repeating over and over again – 'Nevermore!'

Jim Crow

The reign of what became known as 'Jim Crow' served as both a derogatory name for African Americans and the label given to segregationist politics that hardened into law by the first decades of the twentieth century. 'Jim Crow' laws and practices enforced the separation of blacks and whites in public places: in transport and in segregated schools, hospitals, prisons, and even cemeteries.

The name originally came from a minstrel show song and dance devised by Thomas Dartmouth Rice (Daddy Rice) in 1832:

> Wheel about and turn about
> And do jis so,
> Ebry time I wheel about
> I jump Jim Crow.

Sadly, it took another long century and a quarter for America's civil rights movement to begin to turn around the practices and statutes of Jim Crow's rule.

The Raven in Russia

In Russia, writers and artists have portrayed the Holy Fool as an archetype of the simple believers. In his painting *In Russia* (1916), Michael Nesterov portrayed the Holy Fool as the unofficial spiritual leader of the Russian people. He shared certain characteristics with Asian shamans, like the performance of a whirling dance, used also by the Islamic Sufis. Like a shaman, the Holy Fool often used the raven in his rituals. In Russian folklore the raven had a magic and subversive status. Throughout the nineteenth century the peasants of the Volga region saw the Cossack rebel leaders Pugachev and Razin in the form of giant ravens in the sky.

London's Guardians

Ravens are found throughout the Northern Hemisphere, and their range extends further north than any other member of the crow family. They are indigenous to Britain, where their old name *hrafn* has hardly changed since Anglo-Saxon times. Once seen throughout the country, they were driven to remote hills and sea cliffs in the far west and north as their habitat dwindled. Ravens were once common even on the streets of London, in their best scavenging capacity. Now only one small colony survives in London, albeit at a fashionable address. At the Tower of London six ravens – Hardy, Rhys, Larry, Charlie, Hugin, and Munum – are in permanent residence and offer hospitality to two guests, Katy and Cedric. The residents enjoy the undivided attention of their own Yeoman Ravenmaster and a diet of horsemeat and whatever their thousands of tourist admirers also proffer.

An ancient belief would have it that if the ravens should ever leave the Tower, London would be conquered by an enemy. Perhaps that is why the precaution has been taken of clipping their wings! But, no one really knows quite why or when ravens were first associated with the Tower. A Welsh legend dating back to the thirteenth century relates how the head of Bran, whose name means 'raven,' was buried on Tower Hill, facing France. His grave was said to act as a magical charm, which, as long as it lay undisturbed, would protect the country against invasion. Another version of the legend says that an actual raven's head is buried there, and it is a fact that there is a raven burial ground near the Middle Temple! However, it is just possible that the Tower ravens are simply the descendants of birds that were once part of the royal menagerie. Before it was moved to Primrose Hill in 1834, a royal zoo – forerunner of the present London Zoo – had been housed in the Tower for about 500 years.

Whatever the original reason for their presence in the Tower of London, the captive ravens, unable to fulfil their natural inclinations, are a fitting symbol for all the unfortunate people who were once imprisoned within those grim, grey walls.

13

The Robin

Art thou the bird whom man loves best,
The pious bird with the scarlet breast,
Our little English robin?

William Wordsworth (1770–1850)

Stand them side by side and you would never guess that the two birds of the Turdidae family, the American Robin and its European counterpart, were cousins – the one so thrush-like, big, yet slender, the other a little brown ball of a bird with a needle beak. The red breast is the common giveaway. Perhaps the homesick immigrants of the *Mayflower,* seeing the bird's red breast, called it a robin to remind them of home. Yet true to its Linnaean name, *Turdus migratorius,* the American Robin does make rare forays into Europe, while records do not reveal this is ever reciprocated by its less venturesome little cousin.

Wordsworth was right for the Old World – the robin is perhaps the best-loved bird. In England, that nation of gardeners, the robin has a special relationship, because it is the constant companion in any gardening activity, apparently being unafraid of people. John Donne (1572–1631), the celebrated poet, preacher, and dean of St. Paul's in London, recognized this, too, and called it our 'household bird with the red stomacher.' It will perch on a spade handle and fix the gardener with a bright beady eye in the hope that she will soon help it unearth a juicy worm. With a little patient perseverance one can nurture its trust, coaxing it to take food from the hand. In the much-loved children's book *The Secret Garden* by Frances Hodgson Burnett, the grumpy old gardener, Ben Weatherstaff, is entranced by his tame robin: 'they're the friendliest, curiousest birds alive,' says the old man. 'They're almost as friendly as dogs – if you know how to get on with them.'

The earliest recorded evidence we have of a tame robin in Britain comes to us through the delightful story associated with St. Servan, a sixth-century Scottish monk, who lived at Culcross overlooking the Firth of Forth. St. Servan fed the robin daily, cherishing its friendliness. One day some of his pupils, jealous of his favorite scholar, a boy named Kentigern, killed the bird and blamed the death on the favorite. According to the legend, Kentigern picked up the headless body of the little bird and prayed that it should be restored to life; his prayers were answered and saint and robin rejoiced in their old companionship. The literally enchanting end to their story is that when the robin eventually died of old age, all the birds of the air came to join the saint in the singing of the psalms. In later life, Kentigern became a bishop and founded Glasgow Cathedral. To commemorate his early miracle, the Glasgow coat of arms has a robin as one of its heraldic devices.

The European Robin is classified as *Erithacus rubecula*, which means 'solitary little red one.' They do not join flocks, and males and females leave each other after the breeding season. In earlier times it was known as the 'ruddock or ruddy one' and only later given the more specific 'redbreast.'

From the fifteenth century, the Old World redbreast was prefixed by 'robin.' In 1952, the bird officially became just plain 'robin.'

British children have a number of affectionate forenames for popular birds: 'Ralph' Raven; 'Jenny' Wren; 'Jack' Daw; 'Tom' Tit; 'Madge' or 'Mag' Pie; 'Philip' Sparrow; 'Poll' Parrot; 'Jacob' Starling; 'King Harry' Goldfinch; 'Jill' Hooter (any hooting owl); and several more called 'Jack.' In this endearing way, these birds were given special kinship with the human family.

The Westminster Wonder

In 1994 Westminster Abbey produced a CD entitled *Music for Queen Mary*. On it are compositions by Henry Purcell (1659–95), and they cover the short span of the reign of Mary II. He provided music for her coronation on April 11, 1689; for the formal celebration of her birthday on April 30 each year; and for her funeral on March 5, 1694. This small corpus of works includes several masterpieces.

On the cover of the CD is a photo of a robin. At the funeral of Queen Mary in Westminster Abbey, a robin flew around and alighted on her catafalque. He became known as the 'Westminster Wonder.' In the photograph he is shown on the crimson velvet of her crown. Thousands of candles lit an abbey draped in black. The colors illuminated by the candles are set off by the dark soaring vault of the Henry VII Chapel.

The model for the photo of the robin on the cover of the CD had been preserved by a taxidermist. The bird had been found caught in a mousetrap in a farmer's barn in Wiltshire in the winter of 1993, and his accidental death ended in a certain royal photographic immortality.

The Fierce Robin

The European Robin is among the most aggressive of birds, who will attack, often ferociously, any other robin encroaching on its territory and will fight to the death to defend it. The territorial belligerence of our friendly bird was recognized over two millennia ago by Zenodotus, who informed his circle, 'A single bush cannot harbor two robins.'

The Robin as an Ill Omen

It is curious that a bird so well beloved across Europe should sometimes have been regarded as a bird of ill omen. A robin who ventured indoors, for instance, was seen as a portent of impending death; a robin pecking at a window heralded a similar fate for someone in the household. The Reverend Andrew Clark, living in the parish of Great Leighs in Essex, records in his journal on November 16, 1918:

> Theophilus Fuller (aet. 77), Gubbions Green, has died after a very short illness. Great Leighs villagers have a strong belief that attention from a robin is a sign of death. They are now saying, before TF took ill, a robin followed him around for two days. A robin also came in at the window where his daughter (aet. 40) was lying ill with pleurisy. She died this forenoon. A robin hopping about near a villager is more feared than ever.
>
> from *Echoes of the Great War*, the diary of the
> Reverend Andrew Clark between 1914 and 1918

Similarly, the sight of a robin down a coal mine was enough to cause panic among the miners. In 1890 it was reported that one had been seen underground at a colliery near Port Talbot in Wales. Alarmed by the news, the local community assembled to decide what to do, but before action could be taken, an explosion ripped through the pit and 87 miners died.

Robin the Sexton

An old belief, widely held, was that the robin covered over the bodies of the dead with moss and leaves. It acted like the church sexton, one of whose duties was to look after the graveyard and be the gravedigger:

> Call for the Robin Redbreast and the Wren,
>   Since o'er the shady groves they hover
>   And with leaves and flowers do cover
> The friendless bodies of unburied man.
>
> John Webster (ca. 1580–ca. 1634)

So wrote, in Elizabethan times, John Webster in his play *The White Devil*; and Shakespeare also, in *Cymbeline*, refers to the robin 'with charitable bill' covering the dead. Michael Drayton (1563–1631) writes of the bird 'covering with moss the dead's unclosed eye' in his poem 'The Owles.' But the best known is the story of *The Babes in the Wood* in which two children are taken into the woods on the orders of their wicked uncle and left there to die. A robin finds their lifeless bodies, which it then covers over with leaves:

> No burial this pretty pair
> From any man receives
> Till robin redbreast piously
> Did cover them with leaves.
>
> Anonymous, 1595

So in folklore the robin became known as the sexton or gravedigger of the woods. But this long-held version was revised for the pantomine stage, in keeping with the jollity of Christmas festivities, with a happy ending. The Babes are rescued from their untimely fate by another kind of robin – Robin Hood!

To underline the European Robin's acquaintance with death, its song, in late summer and autumn, takes on a plaintive air, a haunting, melancholy note, recalling a funeral lament. In Brittany, this led people to believe that a robin would sing a dirge beside a dead body until it was buried. The poet Robert Herrick shares this hope:

> Laid out for dead, let thy last kindness be
> With leaves and moss-work for to cover me;
> And while the wood nymphs my cold corpse inter,
> Sing thou my dirge, sweet-warbling chorister!
> For epitaph, in foliage, next write this:
> Here, here the tomb of Robert Herrick is.
>
> Robert Herrick (1591–1674)

Robin the Recluse

Although the robin appears in the folklore of France and Germany, in much of Europe the confident bird of the British gardener becomes a shy recluse. Perhaps it has learnt that parts of Europe claim it for the cooking pot, along with most of its other feathered friends, trapping them in nets by the hundred as they make their southward migration for the winter!

In parts of the United States, too, robins were once widely hunted for food. Many were sent to the market because of their fat and juicy flesh.

An ex-governor of Bombay, traveling overland in the nineteenth century, expressed his horror at this indiscriminate gourmandise of goldfinches, nightingales, and robins, exclaiming, 'Our household birds! I would as soon eat a child.' Yet, even in Britain a hundred years ago, robins were caught and caged and sold in the streets. Also, singing competitions were held between rival songsters. All of which incensed William Blake, the visionary poet and painter, and an early 'Green.' He wrote:

A robin redbreast in a cage,
Puts all heaven in a rage.

William Blake (1757–1827)

No doubt similar thoughts helped to inspire those who enacted in British Parliament the Wild Bird Protection Act of 1872, which placed Robin Redbreast, as it was officially called, under legal protection.

The Robin's Nest

The singular nesting sites of European Robins may have contributed to their reputation as loners. They are adept at making their nesting sites in unlikely places: in hats, kettles, hosepipes, the pockets of coats, and many more. Perhaps the oddest was a human skull! In 1796 two men were convicted of mail robbery and were hanged. As was the grisly custom, their bodies were left on the gibbet as an awful warning to others. Years later, a robin nested in the skull of one of them, which led to the following epitaph:

Oh! James Price deserved his fate:
Naught but robbing in his pate
Whilst alive, and now he's dead
Has still robin in his head.

The Frozen Robin

The verses below give witness to popular concern for the robin in winter:

The North Wind doth blow,
And we shall have snow
And what will poor Robin do then?

Poor thing!

He'll sit in a barn,
 And to keep himself warm
Will hide his head under his wing.
                Poor thing!
A traditional song

When the snow is on the ground
  Little Robin Red-breast grieves;
For no berries can be found,
  And on the trees there are no leaves.

The air is cold, the worms are hid,
  For this poor bird what can be done?
We'll strew him here some crumbs of bread,
  And then he'll live till the snow is gone.
Anonymous

The Compassionate Robin

There were various legends about how the robin got his red breast. One story tells of the robin burning itself when bringing the first fire to humans. Another tells of its journey of mercy to the poor souls suffering in the fires of hell to whom it brought drops of water in its beak but was scorched in the process.

A Christian legend offers in winsome fashion an alternative version. On Good Friday a robin flew up on to the cross and tried to ease the pain that Jesus was suffering by pulling out one of the thorns from the crown, which had been cruelly placed on his head. In trying to do this, the chest of the compassionate bird was scratched by the thorn and covered in blood. In another account, it was Jesus's own blood that stained the feathers red. So according to tradition, the robin was regarded as a pious bird, who shared in Christ's sufferings and bears on its breast the signs of his passion.

Who Killed Cock Robin?

This nursery rhyme or folksong was known throughout Europe, although the tasks of the birds vary from country to country:

1) Who killed Cock Robin?
    I, said the Sparrow,
      With my bow and arrow,
    I killed Cock Robin.

2) Who saw him die?
    I, said the Fly,
      With my little eye,
    I saw him die.

3) Who caught his blood?
    I, said the Fish,
      With my little dish,
    I caught his blood.

4) Who'll make his shroud?
    I, said the Beetle,
      With my thread and needle,
    I'll make the shroud.

5) Who'll dig his grave?
    I, said the Owl,
      With my pick and shovel,
    I'll dig his grave.

6) Who'll be the parson?
    I, said the Rook,
      With my little book,
    I'll be the parson.

7) Who'll be the clerk?
    I, said the Lark,
      If it's not in the dark,
    I'll be the clerk.

8) Who'll carry the link?
    I, said the Linnet,
      I'll fetch it in a minute,
    I'll carry the link.

9) Who'll be chief mourner?
    I, said the Dove,
      I mourn for my love,
    I'll be chief mourner.

10) Who'll carry the coffin?
    I, said the Kite,
      If it's not through the night,
    I'll carry the coffin.

11) Who'll bear the pall?
    We, said the Wren,
      Both the cock and the hen,
    We'll bear the pall.

12) Who'll sing a psalm?
    I, said the Thrush,
      As she sat on a bush,
    I'll sing a psalm.

13) Who'll toll the bell?
　　I, said the Bull,
　　　Because I can pull,
　　So Cock Robin, farewell.

14) All the birds of the air
　　　Fell a-sighing and a-sobbing,
　　　When they heard the bell toll
　　For poor Cock Robin.

NOTICE

To all it concerns,
This notice apprises,
The Sparrow's for trial
At next bird assizes.

George Eliot, the pseudonym of Mary Ann Evans, had spent her childhood in the country on farms and writes with personal conviction of rural matters:

> We could never have loved the earth so well if we had had no childhood in it – if it were not the earth where the same flowers come up again and again every spring that we used to gather with our tiny fingers as we sat lisping to ourselves on the grass – the same hips and haws on the autumn hedgerows – the same redbreasts that we used to call 'God's birds,' because they did no harm to the crops.
>
> *The Mill on the Floss* by George Eliot (1819–80)

14

The Sparrow

The origins of the word 'sparrow' are a mixture of Old English and Middle High German, in the words *sparwa* or *sparwe*. In a fourteenth-century English text *hey sugge* means 'hedge sparrow.' The dialect word 'suggie' is still used in parts of rural England.

The *Passer domesticus*, or House Sparrow, is ubiquitous. It is sometimes called the English Sparrow (not to be confused with *Passer montanus*, the Eurasian Tree Sparrow, its more timorous and less obtrusive relation), but it can in fact be found on every continent now, having been introduced where not already native, sometimes with unwelcome results. Both are members of the family of Old World Sparrow. American sparrows (New World sparrows), however, are not closely related to the Old World family.

Nicolas Pike introduced the House Sparrow into Brooklyn in the 1850s: it not only thrived, but proceeded to drive out the native population of Tree Swallows and Bluebirds and proliferated in the city to nuisance proportions. Later, when urban trees in St. Louis, Missouri, were threatened with a leaf-devouring caterpillar (of the snow-white linden moth) that native birds could not control, the House Sparrow was introduced and decimated the caterpillars with immediate effect, but in the process took over St. Louis and moved on to other cities, often riding trains like avian hobos, thus settling across the continent.

The House Sparrow is a colonizing bird; it congregates in easily recognizable chattering flocks, commonplace no matter where you go. It squabbles noisily over its nests and its mates and its repetitive and insistent 'cheep, cheep' gives us scant relief in either street or garden, for it has no other more attractive song in its repertoire. But there are exceptions to this plain song: the North American *Melospiza melodia*, or Song Sparrow, has 20 different melodies and 100 daily variations, which it sings year-long, even caroling in the snow. Another unusual song is found in Cassin's Sparrow, *Aimophila cassinii*, named in 1852 after the Philadelphian naturalist John Cassin. When challenged in the spring, the Cassin's Sparrow soars 20 feet in the air, then descends trilling like a skylark, its head held high, its tail fanned, and its feet reaching for the ground. The Vesper Sparrow, *Pooecetes gramineus*, sings a wild ecstatic melody only at twilight under the evening stars. Not so attractive is the Chipping Sparrow (*Spizella passerina*), a little clay-colored bird nicknamed 'chippy,' whose voice is likened to the buzz of an insect.

As its name implies, the House Sparrow has always found its natural habitat among us, nesting in and alongside human settlements, not only in the eaves of houses but even also in sacred places.

> Even the sparrow finds a home,
>   and the swallow a nest for herself,
>   where she may lay her young,
> at your altars, O Lord of hosts,
>   my King and my God.
> Happy are those who live in your house,
>   ever singing your praise.
>
> Psalm 84:3–4

The Maligned Sparrow

Of all birds, the House Sparrow seems the most maligned and least praised. Even the poets have difficulty in penning a good word for him. William Cowper (1731–1800), a poet of an otherwise perceptive and kindly nature, terms it 'the meanest of the feathered race,' while W. B. Yeats (1865–1939) condemns 'the bawling of a sparrow in the eaves,' and yet another, unnamed poet adds that it is 'thuggish with a dowdy wife.' And so the litany of abuse continues: the sparrow is variously deplored as 'belligerent,' 'lecherous,' 'aggressive,' 'drab,' 'commonplace,' 'undistinguished,' and even just plain 'boring.'

Insulting epithets are the sparrow's bane no matter where. In France we discover in the derivation of the word for sparrow, *moineau*, an unflattering connection – based on numbers and appearance – to *moine*, the word for the monk or friar. A common feature of early modern French life, the monk – either cloistered or mendicant – inspired not reverence but loathing, at least in anticlerical eighteenth-century France. The *moines*, begging in drab habits or living in imagined sumptuous ease in monasteries, were the pariah priests, despised for their taking of alms or tithes that bled the peasant poor. *Un vile moineau* means a disreputable fellow, but literally translates 'a worthless/vile sparrow.'

The German word for sparrow, *Spatz*, is also associated with insolent behavior – or worse – and an old proverb likens the sparrow to an interfering gossip: '*das pfeifen die Spatzen von allen Dächern*' or 'the sparrow twitters from every roof.' However, in Germany even the lowly sparrow, if caught, is proverbially preferred over the 'dove on the roof': *besser ein Spatz in der Hand als eine Taube auf dem Dach* – a more vivid picture somehow than our 'bird in the hand.' To this can be added the mocking diminutive given to the House Sparrow (although not exclusively) in the U.S.: 'LBJ,' initials that stand for 'Little Brown Job' or 'LBB,' 'Little Brown Bird.' This echoes a Victorian diminutive: 'sparrow' was used to mean small change or 'beer money'; for example, when dustmen emptied household bins they were offered 'sparrows' for their trouble.

And when sparrows were not being maligned or diminished, they were being damned with faint praise, as demonstrated in these lines by the Irish poet Francis Ledwidge who wrote:

> There is no bird half so harmless,
> None so sweetly rude as you,
> None so common or so charmless,
> None of virtues nude as you.
>
> But for all your faults, I love you,
> For you linger with us still,
> Though the wintry winds reprove you
> And the snow is on the hill.
>
> Francis Ledwidge (1887–1917)

Identification

To identify the different species of sparrows is made difficult by their close identity of coloring and size. The ornithologist must have a keen eye for slight variations. Unlike many species, the sparrow does not generally alter its appearance in a dramatic fashion to adapt to the environment. It is as though it finds its brown plumage a satisfactory all-purpose, all-place uniform or camouflage. What St. Francis of Assisi wrote of the lark, he could equally as well have written of the sparrow:

> Her clothing – that is her plumage – resembles the earth, and she gives example to Religious that they should not wear soft or colorful garments, but humble in cost and color, as earth is the humblest of the elements.
>
> Francis of Assisi (ca. 1181–1226)

The Son of Venus

During the mating season birds demonstrate distinct behavior patterns, as in the exquisite water dance of certain grebes or the nest making of the Bower Bird. They also mate at a certain time of the year, most often in the springtime.

With sparrows, the mating season continues over many months and is a time of great aggression, the rival cocks in noisy pursuit of each hen, all engaged in frantic chases through the air and in shrubbery and hedges. The resulting unions are fecund with each pairing producing *at least* two broods of up to seven eggs each a year, this despite the casual construction of their somewhat untidy nests.

It was erroneously concluded from this behavior that the sparrow was oversexed, overproductive, and polygamous. Shakespeare's Lucio in *Measure for Measure* warned, a little ironically, 'Sparrows must not build in his house eaves because they are lecherous.' An Elizabethan contemporary, John Lyly (ca. 1554–1606), took a different line, but still added the sparrow to the armory of his Cupid who 'stakes his quiver, bow, and arrow, his Mother's dove, and team of sparrows' in the pursuit of Love. Perhaps he took his cue from Chaucer who, two centuries earlier in his *The Parliament of Foules*, had called the sparrow 'Venus's sone [son].'

Proximity

As a result of living close to us, the sparrow has often fed on cultivated crops of wheat and grain. In Europe in the past huge flocks would be kept at bay by boys who were sent out into the fields with slings and stones, bows and arrows, and nets. 'Sparrower' was the name coined for these sparrow hunters and 'sparrowcide' the term for the mass slaughter of the birds.

Sparrows were also caught for use as a barter element in rents in medieval times, and a rental agreement as late as the sixteenth century bound the tenant to provide 12 'sparouse' in default of anything better.

Before the advent of motor transport, the sparrow relied on the horse and the donkey. Their droppings provided regular urban wayside meals, and their hair provided the birds with an excellent lining for their nests.

Philip Sparrow

The sparrow inspired John Skelton, a witty Norfolk clergy-man, to write a poem on the occasion of the death of his friend's pet sparrow 'Philip' at the hands of Gib the cat. Skelton, perhaps with tongue in cheek, deems the bird's soul to be a worthy item on the prayer list (bede-roll) of the nuns at the convent of Carrow:

> For the soul of Phlypp Sparrow
> That was late slain at Carrow
> Among the Nunnes Black
> For that sweet soules sake
> And for all sparrows' souls
> Set in our bede-rolls,
> *Pater noster qui*
> With an *Ave Mari*.
>
> John Skelton (ca. 1460–1529)

The '*Pater noster qui*' is the opening in Latin of the Lord's Prayer, and the '*Ave Mari*' is the opening of the prayer 'Hail Mary.' The use of the name Philip for the sparrow may derive from the sound of its chirping note or possibly from the Greek *phillipos* which means 'lover of horses,' which we have seen he indeed was.

Sparrows in the Teaching of Jesus

Are not two sparrows sold for a penny? Yet not one of them will fall to the ground apart from your Father. And even the hairs of your head are all counted. So do not be afraid; you are of more value than many sparrows.

Matthew 10:29–31

Mahjong

Mahjong is an old Chinese game usually played by four people. The ivory pieces, either 136 or 144 of them, are called tiles. The noises of these tiles on the board can frequently be heard in the streets of those Chinese houses where the game is in progress. The name of the game derives from *ma*, 'sparrow,' and *djung*, 'play.' When the tiles are rearranged, the sound is called 'the twittering of the sparrows.'

The Cockney Sparrow

'Cockney' originally referred to a so-called cock's egg. If an egg was very small, yokeless and malformed, it was assumed that only a male could have laid it! It was a word used to describe a stupid or spoilt child. Eventually it was used as a name for any foolish person. Country dwellers came to apply it to townspeople because they were ignorant about rural lore and ways.

In the seventeenth century it became restricted to Londoners, particularly to those born within the sound of the bells of St. Mary-le-Bow Church. The inhabitants of London's East End gained a reputation for their sharp wit and their survival instincts in the face of much deprivation. The cheekiness of the sparrow and its once strong urban presence seemed to be reflected in those ebullient characters of the East End.

A comic poem was written in Cockney dialect about a sparrow who had a tough time living up a spout and being savaged by a Sparrow Hawk:

We 'ad a bleed'n' sparer wot
Lived up a bleed'n' spaht,
One day the bleed'n' rain came dahn
An washed the bleeder aht.

An' as 'e layed 'arf drahnded
Dahn in the bleed'n' street
'E begged that bleed'n' rainstorm
To bave 'is bleed'n' feet.

But then the bleed'n' sun came aht –
Dried up the bleed'n' rain –
So that bleed'n' little sparer
'E climbed up 'is spaht again.

But, Oh! the crewel sparer 'awk,
'E spies 'im in 'is snuggery,
'E sharpens up 'is bleed'n' claws,
An' rips 'im aht by thuggery!

Jist then a bleed'n' sportin' type
Wot 'ad a bleed'n' gun
'E spots that bleed'n' sparrer'awk
An' blasts 'is bleed'n' fun.

The moral of this story
Is plain to everyone –
That them wot's up the bleed'n' spaht
Don't get no bleed'n' fun.

                                        Anonymous

15

The Swan

He swells his lifted chest, and backward flings
His bridling neck between his towering wings;
Stately, and burning in his pride, divides,
And glorying looks around, the silent tides:
On as he floats, the silver'd waters glow,
Proud of the varying arch and moveless form of snow.

from 'An Evening Walk' by William Wordsworth (1770–1850)

The swan has an undeniable authority and presence. Its sheer grace, in flight and on the water, has made an indelible imprint on humankind.

Classical Swan

The Greeks were deeply impressed by the swan. The bird was set apart for Apollo, god of light and the arts, and was the chosen creature of all the nine Muses. Indeed, in classical mythology, at Apollo's birth on the isle of Delos, seven pure white swans flew round his birthplace seven times, then bore his chariot north to the land of the Hyperboreans, a place of perpetual sunshine 'at the back of the north wind where the sky is always clear.' So one can perceive why, watching the bird's regular, annual migration south, the beauty of its flight high in the skies in arrowhead formation, dazzling in the light of the sun, the Greeks found in the swan a symbol for all artistic inspiration. And for aesthetic contemplation there was its calm, stately presence on lake and river.

Cygnus, the Latin for swan, was the son of Poseidon (Neptune), the sea god, and at his death was transferred into the night skies, by Apollo himself, to shine on humans perpetually as a star. In another Greek legend, Apollo's father, Zeus, takes the form of a swan to possess the mortal Leda, wife of Tyndareus, king of Sparta. Edmund Spenser, in his *Faerie Queene*, tells the tale in these provocative lines:

> While the proud Bird, ruffling his fethers wyde
> And brushing his fair brest, did her invade,
> She slept: yet twixt her eyelids closely spyde
> How towards her he rusht, and smiled at his pryde.
>
> Edmund Spenser (ca. 1552–99)

From this union, Leda was delivered of two eggs; from the first came Helen of matchless beauty, and from the second sprang the twins Castor and Pollux, known as the *Dioscuri* or 'Sons of God,' renowned warriors. Their births signaled the inevitability of the Trojan War. When Castor was slain in battle, Zeus made the brothers into the constellation Gemini, and together they were honored as the patron and protector of seafarers.

In Acts 28 in the New Testament, strangely, we find an example of this: the boat from Malta in which St. Paul sets out on his passage to Rome has as its figurehead the gods Castor and Pollux. His journey thereafter was uneventful.

Classical writers also imagined that at the death of poets their souls enter the bodies of swans. Thus Virgil is known as 'the Mantuan Swan' and Homer as 'the Swan of Neander.' And more recently, the tradition persists: the flocks of swans on the River Avon never fail to delight the visitors to the town of Stratford, birthplace of the most famous swan of them all, William Shakespeare, whose contemporary playwright Ben Jonson called him 'the Swan of Avon.'

To Further Shores

In northern lands, too, the swan had exerted its fascination. Norsemen were well acquainted with the swan, for both the Bewick and the Whooper species spend their winters in northern Russia and Iceland respectively, while the Mute Swan, the best known of the three, is widespread through the British Isles and around the Baltic Sea. The Norse *skald*, or singer of sacred songs, was also inspired by the swan when he sang his sagas of heroes and dragons and the boundless seas of their adventures. In Icelandic saga we find a ship described as 'the sea king's swan.' Many years later, in 1572, Sir Francis Drake embarked in two small ships to cross the Atlantic and attack the Spanish gold ships sailing from Peru and the Caribbean. Drake's own ship was called *Pasha*; his brother John commanded the other vessel, whose name was *Swan*.

In legend the three *Nornes*, a goddess of three aspects who ruled over the fate of man, was usually depicted as three swans with intertwined necks, representing man's past, present, and future.

In *Beowulf*, the Old English epic related to the sagas, a picturesque name for the sea is 'the swan's riding' or 'way of the swan,' showing that the poet was familiar with the birds' migration paths.

Another Anglo-Saxon poem, 'The Seafarer,' dated to the late sixth century, has these words spoken by a lone sailor adrift on the oceans, perhaps recalling the Whoopers' strange bugle notes, or the beat of the Mute Swan's wings:

> Sometimes I made the song of the wild swan
> My pleasure, or the gannet's call, the cries
> Of curlews for the missing mirth of men.

Swan Song

Swans, despite their association with the god of music, are not usually noted for their sweet voices, even though the Old English word for 'swan' derives from the same root as 'sonnet' and means 'sound.' There are the loud bugles of the Whooper and the constant gabbling of the smaller Bewick, but the more common Mute Swan's voice is most often restricted to mere hisses and grunts. In recognition, in 1768 Thomas Pennant changed the old name 'Tame' to 'Mute.' Yet there has always been the age-long belief that when a swan dies, it sings a hauntingly beautiful death song or threnody:

> The silver swan, who living had no note,
> When death approached, unlocked her silent throat;
> Leaning her breast against the reedy shore,
> Thus sung her first and last, and sung no more:
> 'Farewell all joys, O death come close mine eyes;
> More geese than swans now live, more fools than wise.'
> Anonymous, set as a madrigal by Orlando Gibbons (1583–1625)

Shakespeare took up the theme: 'I will play the swan and die in music,' says Emilia in *Othello*. The bard returns to this theme in *The Merchant of Venice*, when Bassanio, a suitor, is trying to choose the right casket, and Portia, the object of his marriage intentions, calls for music, saying saucily:

> Let music sound while he does make his choice:
> Then, if he lose, he makes a swan-like end,
> Fading on music.

Sir Thomas Browne (1605–82), that collector of arcane lore, in 1646 also subscribed to the idea: 'And on the bankes each cypress bow'd his head/ To heare the swan sing her own epiced (epitaph).' The legend became enshrined in the English language in the expression 'swan song,' meaning a last act or a final piece of creative work. It is a *cause célèbre* among ornithologists who disagree about the factual basis of this belief.

Samuel Taylor Coleridge had no doubts and wittily wrote:

> Swans sing before they die – 'twas no bad thing
> Did certain persons die before they sing.
>
> Samuel Taylor Coleridge (1772–1834)

Plato introduced a different view. He said that the swan, as the sacred bird of Apollo, had the gift of divination and sang not from grief but for joy at the bliss awaiting it in the heavenly realms. Mary Renault, in her novel about the Greek theater *The Mask of Apollo*, puts the following words into Plato's mouth:

> Do you think I have less divination than the swan? For they, when they know they must die, having sung all their lives, sing louder than ever, for joy at going home to the god they serve. Men, who themselves fear death, have taken it for lamentation, forgetting no bird sings in hunger, or cold, or pain. But being Apollo's, they share his gift of prophecy, and foresee the joys of another world.
>
> Mary Renault, *The Mask of Apollo*

There may be an echo of this in Emilianus's statement, 'Cygnus is a fowl most cheerful in auguries.'

In 'The Wild Swans at Coole,' W. B. Yeats saw them also as symbols of an ever-fresh eternal world beyond this earthly one.

Swan Inn

When Coleridge's friend Wordsworth wrote in 'The Waggoner,' 'Who does not know the famous Swan?' it was not an ornithological question. He was referring more mundanely to the Swan Hotel at Grasmere in the Lake District of northern England, where the Lake poets would often meet. In fact, the Swan as an inn sign is common to this day, chiefly because it forms part of the coat of arms of the dukes of Buckingham, a royalist family of immense wealth in land-holdings, which rose to power under the Stuarts.

Black and White

The swan with its white plumage remains a potent symbol of purity, the 'good spirit' of light in popular imagination, as opposed to the 'evil spirit' of darkness and night. An old Scandinavian folktale recorded and retold by Hans Christian Andersen (1805–75) draws on this contrast with a clear theme of redemption and renewal. In *The Traveling Companion*, Andersen tells the story of a maiden bewitched into a black swan, which then performs all manner of foul deeds. However, on being immersed (baptized) three times in clear water, she is washed white in both body and soul, and returns at last to her young husband.

In Ireland, the white swan was shrouded in mystery and magical qualities. It was bad luck to kill one, for the bird could be the host to the soul of a loved one; anyone who committed such a crime would himself die within the year. So it became the guardian symbol of the human soul itself. Russians held the same belief, and that may well have been a factor in the bird's survival there.

In the northern hemisphere it is unlikely that anyone would have seen a black swan until the seventeenth century. They were thought to have been unknown until January 1697, when the Dutch explorer Willem de Vlamingh came across a small flock of these exquisite birds with red beaks and jet-black glossy feathers on an estuary in Western Australia, later known as the Swan River. The *Cygnus atratus*, 'swan clothed in black,' was brought to Europe to wide-eyed amazement; it was on the first list of creatures held at London Zoo; and the Empress Josephine, wife of Napoleon Bonaparte, kept several on the grounds of her palace, Malmaison.

Royal Swan

The Mute Swan is the only swan native to Britain. Claimed to have been introduced by Richard the Lionheart after he returned from the Third Crusade in 1194, an account of 1186 appears to date its establishment to some years before. On September 29th of that year, Hugh of Avalon, a learned Carthusian monk, was enthroned as bishop of Lincoln. An eyewitness reports the arrival of an unusual swan 'such as had never been seen before. . . . He was in truth quite as much larger than a swan than a swan is to a goose; . . . never the less in all things very like a swan especially in colour and whiteness.' The rest of the description adds credence that it was a Whooper cob (*Cygnus cygnus*), strayed out of its migration path. What it points to is that the Mute Swan was already commonplace in Lincoln. The story goes on to tell of the bird's jealous attachment to St. Hugh, while their mutual affection is attested by the emblem on the prelate's coat of arms, a silver swan on a blue background.

Some 900 years ago, another order of monks, the

Benedictines, established what was to become the largest swannery in Europe, at Abbotsbury on the River Fleet in Dorset, whose descendants are still breeding there to this day. It is now the only managed colony of Mute Swans in the world. The flight feathers of these molting swans are made into quills for Lloyd's of London to record ships lost in their 'loss' book.

Edward I also adopted the swan as his heraldic device; on the day of his son's knighthood, as part of the ceremony two swans were brought to Westminster 'gorgeously caparisoned, their beaks gilt.' Another European monarch, Frederick II of Brandenburg, instituted an Order of the Swan to commemorate the legendary knight Lohengrin, the son of Parsival of Grail legend. The betrayed hero was carried along the River Rhine in a skiff drawn by a swan; the bird was in fact the heroine's brother spellbound by yet another evil sorceress. The tale inspired Richard Wagner to compose the eponymous opera, first performed in 1850.

Ownership of swans in Britain was a royal privilege controlled by the crown through 'swanherds' and courts known as 'swan-motes.' During the period of molt, the birds were caught and 'pinioned' (part of a wing amputated) and their beak 'nicked,' or marked with an incision, as a sign of ownership open only to those of high social standing. Today, at the ancient ceremony of 'Swan Upping,' which takes place on the third or fourth Monday in July along the River Thames between London Bridge and Henley, two of the Livery Companies of the City of London, the Dyers and Vintners, celebrate their guardianship under the Crown for the preservation and control of swans, by a single and double nick respectively, while the royal birds remain unmarked. This a more humane advance on the practice of the bishop of Ely in the sixteenth century, who made his claim by eight nicks on the upper mandible, a band across the center and circle near the tip.

Incidentally, the well-known pub sign 'The Swan with Two

Necks' is thought to be a corruption of the Vintner's mark, and should be 'The Swan with Two Nicks.'

Swan ownership was zealously guarded: in 1520, villagers in the East Riding village of Leconsfield were banned from grazing their animals on the Fens for fear of disturbing the swans breeding there. Likewise, the penalties for stealing a swan's egg were heavy: a statute in Henry VII's reign decreed that 'anyone stealing or taking a swan's egg would have one year's imprisonment and make a payment of a fine at the King's will.' For killing a swan in Germany, the culprit had to hang the dead bird by the neck with its tail feathers touching the ground, then cover it entirely with grain, as forfeit.

Swan Entrée

Swans were once popular fare on the menus of the wealthy, and those intended for the table were put into fenced pits containing a 'stew' or pond, to be fattened on barley. One Christmas at the court of Henry II, 125 swans were eaten, which looks insignificant alongside the 400 consumed at the installation of the archbishop of York in 1466. When Lord Spencer (an ancestor of the late Princess Diana) gave a banquet for Charles I at Althorp, the menu included swans in abundance as well as ruff, reeve, redshank, curlew, heron, and many other species besides.

Such a variety of fowl gracing the English table required a fit vocabulary for their carving: for example, you did not carve a goose but 'rear' it, you would 'allay' a pheasant, 'disfigure' a peacock, 'display' a quail, 'thigh' a woodcock or pigeon, 'unbrace' a mallard, and, finally, 'lift' a swan.

Chaucer tells us in his Prologue to *The Canterbury Tales* that his Monk 'a fat swan loved he best of any roast'; he obviously ignored the caveat of the bestiaries against the flesh of the swan because it revealed hypocrisy – the swan being white in outward appearance, but dark inside (the meat of the swan is dark brown in color).

The French word for swan is *cygne*, from which we take our word 'cygnet,' meaning a young swan – this has a culinary implication, for only young birds were considered suitable for those with distinguished palates. Once more it is the French word that dictates our kitchen standards but not our habits, for in 1909 Edward VII proscribed the eating of swan's meat.

Swan Outing

Historically, the luxury trades were swift to realize and exploit the natural endowments of the swan. And not only for its meat was it hunted and harried: even a small Whistling Swan's feathers have been counted to in excess of 25,000, and the plumage of all swans was a highly prized item for numerous trades from bedding to millinery. In the 60 years between 1820 and 1880, the Hudson's Bay Company sold 108,000 swanskins on the London market alone, most of them from Trumpeter Swans; as a result, the species were reduced to a few breeding pairs surviving in Yellowstone National Park. Hundreds of thousands of Black-necked Swans (*Cygnus nigricollis*), a handsome South American species, were killed to make into powder puffs. The Bewick Swan was much in demand for 'the great thickness of very beautiful snow-white down which, when properly dressed by a London furrier, makes beautiful feather boas and other articles of lady's dress of unrivalled beauty.' Even in the 1940s in Russia, the Bewick was still being slaughtered for its down feathers.

Today swans lose their lives mainly through careless ignorance on the part of anglers, who leave lead weights and broken nylon lines in the water, which poison, snag, and injure the birds in great numbers.

Swan Lake and The Dying Swan

One of the most memorable of the metamorphoses of human into swan is that in the story of *Swan Lake* (*Lac des Cygnes*). In this old German folktale, transformed into a ballet by Tchaikovsky, a flock of swans (really spellbound maidens) alights on a lake in the evening and, while reverting to their human form (permitted only in darkness), are discovered by a prince, Siegfried. The ensuing story of love betrayed unfolds to its tragic end, but only after some sublime dancing. Swan maidens are an ideal subject for a classical ballet, with dancers in white gauzy costumes with feathered plume headdresses, floating airily with chorus precision across the stage. They mimic the courtship rituals of real-life swans, in which pairs, which often mate for life, swim together in a dance, heads bobbing and dipping in perfect syncopation, their necks gracefully intertwining.

Nevertheless, the loveliness of the dancing of the ballerinas cannot obscure the fact that it is a deeply dark ballet. The evil Baron von Rothbart, in the form of a terrifying bird of prey, triumphs. The delicate and demure White Swan, Odette, is left by the prince for the manipulative and forceful Black Swan, Odine, daughter of the baron.

The ultimate imitation of a swan in the ballet repertoire was Anna Pavlova's interpretation of it in 'The Dying Swan,' choreographed for her by Fokine. She first danced it in 1907 at a charity performance for poor mothers and their newborn babies. Pavlova, herself the premature daughter of a peasant and a laundress, had known illness and poverty in her own childhood.

Some regarded the dance as a metaphor for her own life. She died prematurely at the age of 50. Her last words to her dresser, as she lay dying, were 'prepare my Swan costume.' The finest tribute her friends and admirers could think of paying her was to play Saint-Saëns's music to an empty stage with the curtain raised. 'The dying flutter of an unseen Swan/ The weeping music and the empty stage.' In Belgium the king and queen and the entire audience stood throughout a similar performance until the orchestra fell silent.

16

The Wren

It is a breathtaking thought that some 600,000 years ago, in the extreme and bitter cold of the Ice Age, a tiny brown bird set out from North America on an extraordinarily arduous journey across the Bering Strait, which was then a land bridge linking America to Asia. The flight was the more remarkable insofar as it went against the normal direction of transcontinental bird movements. That bird, America's Winter Wren, was the ancestor of the European Wren. It is now one of the most widespread of all species, a natural adaptor to its environment, with 297 subspecies in North America alone.

The wren is also remarkable because it seems to attract particularly affectionate attention wherever it is found. In its original North American home, the Pawnee Indians call it 'the happy bird,' and across the Atlantic, in Brittany in France, it is called 'the happy one.' In British climes its minute size inspires names like 'the wee brown button' in the Shetland Isles, 'the mouse's brother' in the not-too-far-distant Faroe Isles, and elsewhere 'Chitty Hen,' 'Titty Wren,' 'Stumpy,' and, the most familiar diminutive of all, 'Jenny Wren.'

But is the affection in which the wren is held sufficient to explain how this tiny creature – against all seeming odds – has triumphed over its disadvantages measured by the evolutionary laws of 'the survival of the fittest?' Despite thriving in so many habitats, the wren appears to have few endowments to ensure its survival: together with the robin and the sparrow, the wren's feeding zone is the one lowest to the ground, making it an easy target for predators, and its nests are fragile and accessible, again increasing its vulnerability. Moreover, the wren's form and flight – even its song – would seem to work against it: its plumage provides little insulation against the cold; its stubby wings are not designed for long flight; and its unmistakable song marks it out immediately to predators – both animal and human. But perhaps the Greeks have given us a clue, for they have always described the wren as 'the elusive one,' their secretive scurrying among the leaves at ground level perhaps a partial explanation for their survival.

The wren has adapted; no matter what the environment, it finds a modus vivendi – from city garden to mountain or moorland or rocky canyon. Its very shortcomings it turns to its advantage: its loud song attracts a mate, so it can reproduce; its nesting creativity both in numbers, choice of site, and construction tend to confuse predators and invite more than one hen bird; the laying of many eggs increases the likelihood of survival; its smallness and plain coloring act as camouflage, permitting it to creep undetected among the undergrowth for its food and give it access to places other birds cannot reach.

A Strange Marriage

> Robin Redbreast and Jenny Wren,
> Are God Almighty's cock and hen.
>
> A traditional song

Their marriage was also celebrated in a children's nursery rhyme, 'The Marriage of Cock Robin and Jenny Wren,' which at its end records thus the climax of their nuptials:

> Then on her finger fair
> Cock Robin put the ring:
> 'You're married now,' says Parson Rook:
> While the Lark 'Amen' did sing.

Still today the wren and the robin share an equal place in our hearts and minds: we know they are both tiny birds, living together in a shared habitat, sourcing their food in close proximity to one another. So perhaps we can understand how they were once seen as appropriate marriage partners. And in another attractive version of the rhyme, we discover details of how Robin courts Jenny, offering her the good things of life – cherry pie and currant wine, which he promises to provide along with colorful clothes like the goldfinch and peacock wear. But Jenny Wren's answer displays her true mettle. To all of Robin's fine talk she replies with almost puritanical candor that she prefers her own modest plumage to his fine fare and frippery:

> Cherry pie is very nice,
> And so is currant wine:
> But I must wear my plain brown gown
> And never go too fine.

It is hard to believe that country folk with their reliable powers of observation could ever have mistaken the robin and wren as male and female of the same species. Perhaps we should seek the source of this confusion in the fascinating but tangled countryside of the imagination, the topography of myths and legends. There we immediately discover some odd goings-on in the poem 'Who killed Cock Robin?' This strange ballad (see also chapter 13) tells us that the chief mourner at Robin's obsequies was not his wife, but the Dove, who says, 'I mourn for my love.' In this tale poor Jenny Wren, his bride and the unwitting cause of his demise, is strangely reduced to the role not of grieving widow, but of pallbearer! Her husband's death, it seems, has been the consequence of an unseemly scene between the Cuckoo who had 'caught hold of Jenny and pulled her about,' provoking the Sparrow to take aim at the Cuckoo, missing him and transfixing poor Robin instead.

We do not expect consistency when reading legends. Certainly, in folklore, the two birds sometimes overlap or exchange roles. Some legends say the robin first brought fire down to earth, while some opt for the wren. In still other versions, the birds divide the task between them – the robin takes the burning brand from the wren for the last part of the journey, and it is then that he scorches his breast. These variations may well have come about by a gradual merging of different folkloric traditions, those of Britain and northern France with those from the Mediterranean countries.

The King of the Birds

Throughout Europe, for 2,500 years fable has recognized but one King of the Birds. It was not, as we might imagine, the mighty eagle, but rather the tiny brown bird that we glimpse darting busily in and out of nooks and crannies in search of its insect food. The wren derives its Latin name, *Troglodytes troglodytes*, which translates 'cave-dweller,' from its habit of living in holes in walls and trees. It would thus seem to us an odd choice as king until we search the literature.

There we find the old legend of the Parliament of Birds. A meeting called to decide who would be their king agreed that the bird that could fly the highest would be granted this illustrious title. A contest was arranged and, as all the other birds fell away, it looked as if the eagle was the clear and undisputed winner. But the little wren had cunningly hidden itself in the great bird's feathers! Just as the exhausted eagle reached its limit, out popped the wren and fluttered a little higher, crying, 'Birds, look up and see your king.' So though achieved through trickery and deceit (often laudable attributes in legendary heroes such as Odysseus), the wren won the coveted title.

The bird's legendary cunning is reflected in its name. In Old English, words beginning with 'wr' indicate twisting or perversity: writhe, wriggle, wring, wrist (the twisting joint), wreathe (flowers or leaves twisted together), wrench.

In many European languages the bird's name reflects its royal role: *Roitelet* ('kinglet' or 'little king') in French; in Swedish, *Kungs fogel* ('king's bird'); *Zaunkönig* ('hedge king') or *Schneekönig* ('snow king') in German; and *Dru-ien* (king of the birds) in Welsh. The wren's majesty is recognized in such tales as the Grimm brothers' 'Der Zaunkönig und der Bär' (The Wren and the Bear), in which all four-footed animals go into battle against the creatures of the air – and the wren's troops win because of a trick.

It has been suggested that the title of 'king' belonged originally to the even smaller Goldcrest, because of its distinctive head markings – a black-bordered, orangey-yellow crest that the male raises during courtship displays, and because its name in some languages implies kingship. This bird's scientific name is *Regulus regulus*, the Latin for 'ruler.' Only 3½ inches long, Britain's smallest bird is known in some parts of the country as the Goldcrested Wren, but it is not in fact a member of the wren family, Trogolytidae. So the wren retains its royal pretensions, exclusively, if somewhat deceptively.

Hunting the Wren

He who shall hunt the Wren
Shall never be beloved of men.

William Blake (1757–1827)

In spite of Blake's couplet, the wren for centuries was the victim of an elaborate yearly ritual. For most of the year it was left to live its life undisturbed. It was even held sacred by some people, so that killing one or robbing its nest was said to bring certain ill-luck: 'Hunt a robin, hunt a wren, / Never prosper boy or man,' ran an old Cornish rhyme. But at Christmas time, between December 26 or St. Stephen's Day (named for the first Christian martyr) and January 6 (Epiphany or Twelfth Night), a favorite pastime was 'Hunting the Wren.' In their ritual, one or more of the little birds were flushed out from their winter roost by gangs of boys, killed, mounted on a pole, and then ceremoniously paraded through the streets. Sometimes the bird was just captured, placed in an elaborate open 'wren cart' or receptacle, tied with ribbons and paraded around unharmed. But generally it was killed, its persecutors going to absurd, prescribed lengths to carry this out – 'with sticks and stones' or 'with bows and arrows.' One wren hunting song went so far as to stipulate that 'great guns and cannons' were to be used for the chase and that the wren's tiny corpse should be cut up 'with hatchets and cleavers' before being 'boiled in brass pans and cauldrons.' Folktales justified this cruel event with apocryphal stories such as that the wren had led Jesus Christ's enemies to him in the Garden of Gethsemane, or that it had alerted the guards when St. Stephen tried to escape. And in southern Ireland the wren was condemned for warning Cromwell's soldiers that the Irish were advancing on them.

Until well into the nineteenth century, wren hunting continued to flourish in Wales and the Isle of Man, and also in a number of English counties, particularly in the south and west. In parts of France also there were elaborate formalized rituals in which even the church took part. The custom lingered on for many more years in southern Ireland. 'Wren Boys' with blackened faces, or sometimes dressed in girls' clothes, would beg round a neighborhood with a hat, calling 'Give us a penny to bury the wren.' Fortunately, as time went

on, the 'wren' became just a potato with a feather stuck in it.
A traditional 'Wrenning Song' entreated:

> The wren, the wren, king of all the birds,
> On St. Stephen's Day was caught in the furze.[1]
> Come, give us a bumper,[2] or give us a cake,
> Or give us a copper[3] for charity's sake.

[1] a gorse bush [2] a glass of something to drink [3] the old British penny coin

It is most likely that these rites date back to the Bronze Age,
when end-of-year orgies (Dionysia) climaxed in killing a 'peasant' king to ensure fertility and good fortune for the community. The wren was the bird sacred to Dionysus, god of wine.

The Nest Builder

The wren is an enthusiastic and energetic nest builder – he is
never content with just a single work of art; indeed, the Marsh
and Sedge Wrens construct at least a dozen nests, and often 20
or more! Their nests are exquisitely woven constructions,
dome-shaped, built variously of moss, leaves, and grasses.
Wrens site their delicate nests in every conceivable hiding
place, from cacti and thorny bushes (the Cactus Wren),
canyons and chimneys (the Canyon Wren), to hedgerows and
shoes, mechanical machinery, and even, as the legend of St.
Malo tells us, in a cloak just discarded by the saint.

The speed of construction is remarkable, too; normally, the
male will take just one single day to complete the external
frame. These enticing structures are then offered up to the
female who is allowed to select the one that is to be her home.
The cock bird entices her with veritable bouquets of song, display, dance, and conducted tours, or even, in the case of the
Fairy Wren in Australia, with an actual single flower bouquet
offered to her in its beak. Having graciously deigned to make

her choice of nest, the female then lines it with feathers – literally 'feathering her nest' – and lays up to a dozen eggs. Any other nest is termed a 'cock's nest' and may be used for roosting, as decoy, or just discarded as obsolescent. Two broods of eggs are usual. The female does all the incubating, although the male may take a clutch to one of the rejected nests while the female attends to the other.

The male may also go polygamous and invite a second female into another of the nests. The Saxon word for wren was *wroene*, meaning 'lascivious,' which may well indicate that the male wren's inclinations were remarked upon from early times. Wrens obviously follow the advice not 'to put all your eggs into one basket.' An old rhyme attests to the wren's nurturing skills, relating how she purposely promotes success-ful progeny by laying a surprising number of eggs:

> Coo-coo-coo
> It's as much as a pigeon can do
> To bring up two.
> But the little wren can maintain ten,
> And keep them all like gentlemen.

Adult male wrens are, however, less than gentlemanly in maintaining their territorial rights.

The Rock Wren of the West builds not just an elaborate nest, but a remarkable landscape feature too. It lays beauti-fully arranged pebbles to make a path some 8 to 10 inches long, which leads to the nest's entrance. There it erects a small wall and then paves the bottom of the nest with hundreds of other pebbles, some up to 2 inches long, which it mingles with feathers and other decorative features. (One such nest con-tained 1,791 items, including screws, tacks, pins, paper clips, pen nibs, and toothpicks!)

The wren does indeed have a place in God's creation, estab-lished through the very seeming disadvantages with which it was endowed. There is a universal lesson here.

17

Bird Illustrators

Among the 'mutual charities' practiced between humans and birds is the art of book illustration. As far back as 2500 BCE, the Egyptians used birds as picture symbols in their hiero-glyphic writing; later, in Celtic culture birds are integral to the graceful interwoven lines of its art and demonstrate a new imaginative vigor. Birds, too, perched in the delicate borders of illuminated manuscripts of Europe in the fourteenth and fifteenth centuries, with artists more ready to copy birds from nature. For the bird artist then as now the real test is to match an accurate ornithological record of a bird with an aesthetic presentation that can stand on its own merits. This required a combination of scientific accuracy and artistic skills that was to evolve over many centuries.

Francis Willoughby and John Ray were early in the field, with their pioneering *Ornithologia* of 1676. And when the third duke of Richmond, ambassador to the court of Louis XV of France, visited the Sèvres porcelain factory in 1765 to order a complete dinner service for himself, he took with him the recently published work of George Edwards, *A History of Birds*, so the French artists could copy his English favorites (the complete set is still at his family seat, Goodwood House, Sussex). The great French naturalist the comte de Buffon fur-ther elaborated this marriage of artistry and ornithology with his 44-volume *Histoire naturelle*, of which 9 volumes are devoted to birds. But bird illustration would reach its apogee in America during the eighteenth and nineteenth centuries fol-lowing the opening up of the continent to settlers by the early explorers, surveyors, and mapmakers. These pioneers were joined by a new breed of artist-naturalist, eager both to procure specimens and to record them – before they were consigned to the stockpot!

There were many problems. The artists had to be adventurous, accurate, and adaptable in order to paint the birds. Photography had not yet been invented, trapping and sketching were inadequate, and so to freeze-frame specimens for painting these artists' only resort was most often to shoot their subject matter. Without refrigeration the birds also had to be instantly skinned, gutted, and later stuffed in order to preserve them as fit models for the artist – despite the inevitable damage incurred and the lackluster colors of a corpse. The artists had the additional problem of finding publishers willing to accept the financial and technical risks involved. Often public subscription was the only answer and had to be advertised and solicited, a long and arduous demand on the artists' energies. To reproduce the originals, artists had to master the art of etching or engraving or else entrust their pictures to a journeyman craftsman who might well fall short of the aesthetic qualities needed.

We can see an early example of the work of a bird artist in the accurate but somewhat stilted hand-colored engravings of Mark Catesby (1683–1749), an English botanist and engraver, living first in Virginia and then Carolina, who produced in 1731 a *Natural History of Carolina, Florida and the Bahama Islands*, the first published account of North American fauna and flora (the original watercolors are preserved in the Royal Library at Windsor in Britain). He was, however, with George Edwards, a pioneer in the field, and Catesby was the first artist to use folio-sized illustrations in his books and accompanied his engravings with texts full of keen observations. His patron was Sir Hans Sloane, whose own collection, augmented by Catesby, was to form the basis of the British Museum, which occupied Sloane's mansion, Montague House, in London; the nature specimens would later be transferred to the present Natural History Museum in London.

Catesby helped to motivate the Scottish-born Alexander Wilson (1766–1813), an autodidact who became a prominent naturalist and combined scientific observation with a skilled but less conspicuous talent in drawing. His *American Ornithology* – of which the first of 8 completed volumes was published in 1804, with Thomas Jefferson among the subscribers – depicts 264 species of the 343 birds found on the continent at that time, with no less than 48 being his own discoveries. It was a commercial triumph and put America on the world map with its own peculiar avifauna and with their own names and classifications.

On one of his ornithological expeditions Wilson visited Louisville, Kentucky, where he met the Haitian-born John James Audubon (1785–1851) whose bird drawings may well have inspired him. Audubon had for many years been drawing the birds of the countryside of his father's farm near Philadelphia. It was he, and not Wilson, who was to develop the full potential of the art of bird illustration, in his *Birds of America*. 1827 saw the first plates produced, with the last of the four volumes published in 1838. Larger than life himself, Audubon's prints are extravagant in size (double elephant folio paper, 27" x 40") and opulently colored, but they are marked by an admirable accuracy, and a freedom of form and design, of sweep and scope, which have never been surpassed. And they are matched by his remarkable prose commentaries, which are packed with information, cross-references, and detailed observation, as well as being evocative word pictures in themselves. For instance, his hummingbird is a 'glittering fragment of the rainbow.' And his descriptions of habit and territory, in this instance for the mockingbird, are equally spellbinding:

> It is where Nature seems to have paused, as she passed over the earth, and opening her stores to have strewed with unsparing hand the diversified

> seeds from which have sprung all the beautiful and
> splendid forms. . . . [It is] there that the Mocking
> Bird should have fixed her abode, there only that
> its wondrous song should be heard.

Audubon had gone to England in 1826 to raise subscriptions,
where he had an instant appeal with his romantic, wilderness
background – he was known as 'The American Woodsman' –
and was fortunate to gain the patronage of the bird-loving
King George IV and the friendship of Sir Walter Scott.
Following in the footsteps of Benjamin Franklin (who was the
Royal Society's first American fellow), Audubon was elected a
fellow of the Society in London. He easily secured a publisher.
He was also able to publish in America in 1842 a popular edition of his great work.

He realized a long-cherished ambition by visiting the
Northumberland workshop of Thomas Bewick (1755–1828),
who combined the skills of artist-engraver and field naturalist
as never before. Bewick's greatest achievement was the publi-
cation of his *British Birds* (1797–1804) in which his drawings
were so close to nature and his engravings so accurate (on the
end-grain of hardwood) that they were thereafter emulated by
most illustrators. His renown was such that both a swan and
a wren were named after him.

Bewick was the major influence on John Gould (1804–81),
widely traveled, prolific, and the most financially successful
of all the bird illustrators. Starting employment as a taxidermist, he acquired great prestige in 1829, when he stuffed a
camel – the gift of Mehemet Ali, pasha of Egypt, to George
IV – which sadly had never recovered from the rigours of the
sea voyage. Gould had learnt that arsenic was the essential
ingredient in preservation and helped usher in a new era of
taxidermy in which, although the life of the specimen was
prolonged, that of the taxidermist was put at great toxic risk.
(Only a handful of bird specimens survive from before 1830.)
He had become a keen ornithologist and subsequently was

appointed the first curator and preserver at the museum of the London Zoological Society. His appointment allowed him entrée to all the great bird collections, and it was he who alerted Darwin to the significance of the subtle variations among the Galapagos finches – Darwin had thought they were wrens – and so gave him the first inkling of the transmutation of species and from that his theory of evolution. After specimen-seeking travels in Africa, Australia, and Europe, Gould eventually came to America – he wanted to see at first hand a live hummingbird, the bird which had first inspired him to take up illustration! To his great joy he found them in numbers in Washington, DC. A great part of the John Gould archives is housed in the Spencer Research Library of the University of Kansas.

Taxidermy would continue to play a crucial role for the bird illustrator, and J. G. Bell's taxidermy shop on Broadway and Worth Street in New York was a center for it. Bell had once traveled with Audubon searching for specimens and remained his friend and taxidermist. Visitors to the shop included the explorer and naturalist Titian Peale (1799–1885), also a bird illustrator, whose father founded the Philadelphia Museum (and named all his sons after Renaissance painters). Peale provided the illustrations for the revised version of Wilson's *American Ornithology* which would be published by Napoleon's nephew Charles Lucien Bonaparte between 1825 and 1832. The young Theodore Roosevelt learned to skin birds in Bell's shop, and there too, no doubt, imbibed his great love for the natural

world, which led him as president to do more for wildlife in the United States than any of his 24 predecessors in the presidency.

Final mention must go to the New Yorker Roger Tory Peterson (1908–1996) who first created the inexpensive field guide to bird recognition. Alongside detailed texts, he arrowed the key diagnostic features in a clear if formalized style of color illustration, which was a major breakthrough in bird identification. He produced field guides both for the United States and then for Britain and Europe.

The present-day Audubon Society, founded in the late 1800s by, among others, the aptly named George Bird Grinnell (who had been tutored by Audubon's wife, Lucy), is with its many state branches and its positive action for the protection and preservation of birds and other wildlife in their habitats a fitting and lasting tribute to all these artist natural-ists who braved the wilderness in their love of birds, to observe, to record, and to paint them.

18

State Birds

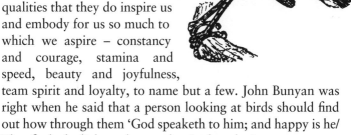

It is a measure of how deeply embedded birds are in our sensibility that we wish to identify them with our home states (and likewise with some of our professional sports teams – including hawks and cardinals, falcons, ravens, and eagles). It is also a tribute to their enduring qualities that they do inspire us and embody for us so much to which we aspire – constancy and courage, stamina and speed, beauty and joyfulness, team spirit and loyalty, to name but a few. John Bunyan was right when he said that a person looking at birds should find out how through them 'God speaketh to him; and happy is he/ That finds the light and grace that in them be.'

Frequently it is the schoolchildren of a state who have nominated a bird to symbolize their state. The children's choice will probably be dictated by the bird they see or hear most often. Sometimes a bird, such as the Eastern Bluebird, will be chosen for its outstanding beauty, or as with its cousin the Mountain Bluebird, because of its special or exclusive association with a state or region. But the choice of some of the state birds arises from more uncommon reasons, as mentioned below.

Baltimore Oriole – Maryland

Blue Hen Chicken – Delaware

Brown Pelican – Louisiana

Brown Thrasher – Georgia

Cactus Wren – Arizona

California Gull – Utah

California Valley Quail – California

Cardinal – Illinois, Indiana, Kentucky, North Carolina, Ohio, Virginia, West Virginia

Chickadee – Maine, Massachusetts

Common Loon – Minnesota

Eastern Bluebird – Missouri, New York

Eastern Goldfinch – Iowa, New Jersey

Great Carolina Wren – South Carolina

Hermit Thrush – Vermont

Lark Bunting – Colorado

Mockingbird – Arkansas, Florida, Mississippi, Tennessee, Texas

Mountain Bluebird – Idaho, Nevada

Nene Goose – Hawaii

Purple Finch – New Hampshire

Rhode Island Red Hen – Rhode Island

Ring-necked Pheasant – South Dakota

Roadrunner – New Mexico

Robin – Connecticut, Michigan, Wisconsin

Ruffed Grouse – Pennsylvania

Scissor-tailed Flycatcher – Oklahoma

Western Meadowlark – Kansas, Montana, Nebraska, North Dakota, Oregon, Wyoming

Willow Goldfinch – Washington

Willow Ptarmigan – Alaska

Yellowhammer (Yellow-shafted Flicker) – Alabama

The Wood Thrush is the official bird of the District of Columbia.

When Meriwether Lewis and William Clark set out on their epic 8,000-mile journey which lasted almost 3 years (1804–06) to explore and map the American West, they were asked by Thomas Jefferson to send back information on the fauna and flora of the regions through which they traveled. On June 21, 1805, they reported the sighting of the 'Old Field Lark' – our present Western Meadowlark, which, after the Cardinal, is the most popular state bird. Jefferson's request has left a substantial legacy because all the states that now carry the Western Meadowlark as their state bird lie – more or less – along the route of the Lewis and Clark expedition across the continent.

The striking black and orange colors of the Baltimore Oriole match the colors on the coat of arms of George Calvert, Lord Baltimore, the seventeenth-century proprietor of the province of Maryland, and that was how the association first began. The birds so impressed the early settlers that when in 1698 they were royally commanded to send back to England 'Beasts of Curiosity,' the Orioles were their first choice for the royal gardens of their majesties.

Land-locked Utah seems to have made an odd choice of its state bird in the California Gull. The explanation for honoring the bird lies in a miraculous event. In 1848 Mormons were struck by an invasion of Rocky Mountain crickets. Huge swarms of the insects descended on the state and devoured hundreds of acres of crops. What threatened to be a disaster was mysteriously averted by the sudden appearance of flocks of seagulls that feasted on the crickets with such gusto and application that both the sated birds and the devoured crickets disappeared as suddenly as they came. In Salt Lake City a seagull monument commemorates this 'miracle of the gulls.'

There are only two domestic fowls in the list, the Rhode Island Red Hen and the Blue Hen. The latter was chosen because during the Revolutionary War men who had been recruited in Kent County, Delaware, brought the legendary fighting Blue Hen cocks with them, and when not themselves fighting staged cockfights. The fierceness of the birds was said to be matched by the soldiers' own consequent bravery in battle, and so the bird became forever identified with Delaware. Whereas the Rhode Island Red Hen was chosen by that state as it had been bred there from chickens, and as a breed achieved an international reputation as a prime farmhouse egg-layer and meat provider.

Vermont's Hermit Thrush has a wider connection: when Walt Whitman wrote his elegy on the death of President Abraham Lincoln, 'When Lilacs Last in the Dooryard Bloom'd,' he chose this shy little bird with its continuously lilting song as his symbol of life-in-death. For Whitman, the bird represented a promise, just as the lilacs did, that the president would live on in a spiritual existence, an ever-renewing source of inspiration and hope. The poet had transformed the Hermit Thrush's voice into the voice of America itself.

19

Birdsong

That's the wise thrush; he sings each song twice over
Lest you should think he never could recapture
   the first fine careless rapture!

'Home Thoughts from Abroad' by Robert Browning (1812–89)

Walt Whitman claimed his whole life was changed by hearing, as a boy, the song of a bird at night, breaking its heart in longing for its lost mate. 'Now I know what I am for,' he cried. He described how this affected him:

Never more shall I escape, never more the
   reverberations,
Never more the cries of unsatisfied love be absent
   from me,
Never again leave me to be the peaceful child I was
   before what there in the night,
By the sea under the yellow and sagging moon,
The messenger there arous'd, the fire, the sweet
   hell within,
The unknown want, the destiny of me.

Walt Whitman (1819–92)

Our landscape is desolate without birdsong. John Keats, to describe a scene of desolation in his poem 'La Belle Dame Sans Merci,' wrote:

Oh, what can ail thee, Knight at arms,
   Alone and palely loitering?
The sedge has wither'd from the lake,
   And no birds sing.

John Keats (1795–1821)

While Milton, to capture the sweetness of dawn in Paradise, fills it with the 'charm' (Middle English *cearm*, 'birdsong') of earliest birds.

There are some 4,000 songbirds or passerines of the order Passeriformes. Birds generally sing in order to make territorial claims. Gilbert White noted that each bird has a number of different calls, but not all species are equally eloquent.

> Some are copious and fluent in their utterance, while others are confined to a few important sounds; no bird, like the fish kind, is quite mute, though some are rather silent. The language of birds is very ancient, and like other ancient modes of speech, very elliptical: little is said, but much is meant and understood.
>
> Gilbert White (1720–93)

Very few species sing continuously throughout the day. Daybreak in springtime produces the peak period for birdsong; the dawn chorus starts well before sunrise. The wren's song is astonishingly loud and robust and would seem to be its only natural claim to kingliness. Its diminutive body can scarce contain the quality and quantity of sound that comes from it, which, it is claimed, can be heard at a distance of some 650 yards. 'Bursting into song' is therefore an apt description, as the wren pours forth its 103-note phrase at such speed that this musical ripple of nine seconds' duration is only intelligible to the human ear as a tune when it is recorded and played back slowly.

Gilbert White on Birdsong

On the variety of song, Gilbert White wrote in *The Natural History of Selborne* (1789):

> The notes of the eagle kind are shrill and piercing. Owls hoot in a fine vocal sound, much resembling the *vox*

humana [human voice]; they also use a quick call and a horrible scream; and they can snort and hiss when they mean to menace. Ravens, beside their loud croak, can exert a deep and solemn note that makes the woods to echo; the amorous sound of a crow is strange and ridiculous; rooks, in the breeding season, attempt sometimes in the gaiety of their hearts to sing, but with no great success; doves coo in amorous and mournful manner; the woodpecker sets up a sort of loud and hearty laugh; the fern-owl or goat-sucker, from dusk to daybreak, serenades his mate with the clattering of castanets. . . . Aquatic and gregarious birds, especially the nocturnal, that shift their quarters in the dark, are very noisy and loquacious; as cranes, wild geese, wild ducks, and the like; their perpetual clamour prevents them from dispersing and losing their companions.

The Singing Diva

Maybe no bird can compete with the nightingale (*Luscinia megarhynchus*) as a source of inspiration to poets, among whom figure Matthew Arnold, Samuel Coleridge, Edmund Gosse, John Keats, Andrew Marvell, Christina Rossetti, Alfred Tennyson, and William Wordsworth, in English poetry alone. On a calm night the song of the nightingale can carry for up to a mile. In East Anglia it was called the barley-bird because its song was first heard when the barley was being sown. The nightingale's name comes from the Saxon *niht-galan* meaning 'to sing at night.'

Alcuin, who was born about 735 in York and died in 804, became the abbot of Tours in 796 and an adviser on religious and educational matters to Charlemagne. One bit of advice he offered was that the nightingale's constant urge to sing illustrated how worship should perpetually ascend to God.

Nightingales sing as lovers, not merely as property claimants. Although they sing during the daytime, it is by night that their concerts are most impressive. Their song inspired Manning Shirwin and Eric Maschwitz to write the music and words for a most romantic song, which the actress Judy Campbell made famous. Set in London's West End, it recaptured a perfect moment of night romance. There was a celestial smile; there were angels dining at the Ritz; and 'a nightingale sang in Berkeley Square.'

Far from Berkeley Square, nightingales are thought to be stimulated to sing by the sound of music. In Afghanistan, caged birds are sometimes brought to musical performances. The interwoven sounds of music and birdsong create for Afghans a concert of rare delight.

The singing of all birds has for them a sacred dimension. Each species in its own way sings of the many names of God. The Sufis regard birdsong as a form of Zikr or the Recollection of God. Therefore, birds forever proclaim the preeminence of God. The same belief is found in the canticle *Benedicite, omnia opera*:

> O all ye Fowls of the Air, bless ye the Lord:
> Praise him, and magnify him for ever.

A Dawn Chorus High Mass

David Ap Gwylym, a medieval Welsh poet, was so awestruck by one dawn chorus that he saw it as an act of divine worship, a High Mass celebrated by bird choristers:

> This morning, lying couched amid the grass
> In the deep, deep dingle south of Llangwyth's Pass,
> While it was yet neither quite bright nor dark,
> I heard a new and wonderful High Mass.
> The chief priest was the nightingale: the lark
> And thrush assisted him: and some small bird
> (I do not weet his name) acted as Clerk.

My spirit was sapped in ecstasy: each word,
Word after word, thrilled through me like the deep
Rich music of a dream: not wholly asleep
Nor all awake was I, but, as it were,
Tranced somewhere between one state and the other.
All heavy thoughts that through the long day smother
Man's heart and soul with weariness and care
Were gone, and in their place reigned pure delight.
The nightingale, sent from a far and bright
Land by my golden sister, prophesied
Of blessed days to come, in a sweet voice:
And the small bird, responding, sang 'Rejoice, rejoice!'
I heard his little bill tinkle and jingle
With a clear silver sound that filled the dingle.
Heaven is a state wherein bliss and devotion mingle,
And such was mine this morn: I could have died
Of Rapture. . . .

David Ap Gwylym (fourteenth century)

Philomela

John Pecham was born at Patcham in Sussex in about 1225. When he taught in Rome his reputation was so formidable that even the cardinals rose from their seats and uncovered their heads as he entered the room. He died in Mortlake on December 8, 1292, having been a great reforming archbishop of Canterbury. He is buried in Canterbury Cathedral. Among his many interests, science and philosophy figured highly – besides his theology of which some 14 works have survived. He was also no mean versifier; among his poems is one to 'Philomela,' the nightingale.

The legend of Philomel recounts her rape, tongue-cutting and terrible revenge. In Ovid's version of the story she is changed into a nightingale by the gods as she flees her abuser. So great was her sorrow that she sang while pressing her

breast against a thorn. Despite many other melancholy inter-
pretations of the nightingale's song, Socrates in contrast chose
in the *Phaedo* to depict the nightingale singing for joy, and
Chaucer referred to the merry nightingale.

Pecham's poem was not the first in British poetry in which
the nightingale appeared. The first known allusion to it was in
a seventh-century poem 'Aenigmata' by St. Aldhelm, first
bishop of Sherborne. In this poem the bird's return in spring
was seen as symbolizing the resurrection of Jesus Christ.

A Thousand Years and a Day

There is a German legend about a monk called Brother Felix,
who while meditating on the psalms found he could not
understand the phrase in Psalm 90, 'For a thousand years in
thy sight are but as yesterday.' How could so many years be
as one day? He ventured into a forest and then he heard birdsong. Henry Longfellow takes up the story:

> And lo! He heard
> The sudden singing of a bird,
> A snow-white bird, that from a cloud
> Dropp'd down,
> And among the branches brown
> Sat singing
> So sweet, and clear, and loud,
> It seem'd a thousand harp-strings ringing.
> And the monk Felix closed his book,
> And long, long
> With rapturous look
> He listened to the song,
> And hardly breathed or stirr'd.

So he listens and listens and listens, until he suddenly remem-
bers he must go to the monastery for Vespers. But when he

returns all is changed; there are new faces everywhere, in refectory and choir. What could have happened? He enquires of the librarian, who recalls the name Felix as one who had been there many years before. He brings out the roll of all the monks who have ever belonged to the monastery. They find:

> That on a certain day and date,
> One thousand years before,
> Had gone forth from the convent gate
> The Monk Felix, and never more
> Had entered that sacred door:
> He had been counted among the dead.
> And they knew at last
> That, such had been the power
> Of that celestial and immortal song,
> A thousand years had pass'd,
> And had not seem'd so long
> As a single hour.
>
> Henry Longfellow (1807–82)

Brother Felix had been enthralled by the song of a bird for a thousand years, surpassing Orpheus and the charms of his lyre.

The Vain Quest

The idea, pushed to absurdity, that we are what we eat is not new. Certain ancient Greeks, not having strong black coffee, ate the flesh of nightingales to stay awake. Was not the bird a night performer? The Greeks also ate the tongues of nightingales to acquire a talent for singing. The Romans could be equally absurd. The rich son of Aesopus Claudius, the great Roman tragic actor and spendthrift of the first century CE, once spent 100,000 sesterces on a dish composed of the tongues of birds famous for their song or imitative power – such was his desire to obtain his father's and master's voice.

As late as the first half of the twentieth century, Turkish children who were slow in speaking were made to eat the tongues of what were considered talkative birds.

The Real Thing

The courtiers of a certain Spartan king were always anxious to distract him from the heavy duties of state. One day they found a small boy who could perfectly imitate the song of the nightingale. They hastened to bring the boy to the king for his entertainment, but having informed him of the boy's exceptional talent, they were told, quite kindly, to send him away. 'Thank you,' said the king, 'but, you see, I have heard the nightingale itself.'

Hans Christian Andersen unfolds a similar idea in his magical tale 'The Nightingale,' in which the emperor of China comes to understand, as he faces death, that the most refined mechanical bird will never match the beauty of the real bird's song:

> Death continued to stare at the emperor with his cold, hollow eyes, and the room was fearfully still. Suddenly there came through the open window the sound of sweet music. Outside, on the bough of a tree, sat the living nightingale. She had heard of the emperor's illness, and was therefore come to sing to him of hope and trust. And as she sung, the shadows grew paler and paler; the blood in the emperor's veins flowed more rapidly, and gave life to his weak limbs; and even Death himself listened, and said, 'Go on, little nightingale, go on.'
>
> 'Then will you give me the beautiful golden sword and that rich banner? and will you give me the emperor's crown?' said the bird.
>
> So Death gave up each of these treasures for a song; and the nightingale continued her singing. She sung of the quiet graveyard, where the white roses grow, where the

elder-tree wafts its perfume on the breeze, and the fresh, sweet grass is moistened by the mourners' tears. Then Death longed to go and see his garden, and floated out through the window in the form of a cold, white mist.

'Thanks, thanks, you heavenly little bird. I know you well. I banished you from my kingdom once, and yet you have charmed away the evil faces from my bed, and banished Death from my heart, with your sweet song. How can I reward you?'

'You have already rewarded me,' said the nightingale. 'I shall never forget that I drew tears from your eyes the first time I sang to you. These are the jewels that rejoice a singer's heart. But now sleep, and grow strong and well again. I will sing to you again.'

Hans Christian Andersen (1805–75)

Music and Birdsong

The connection between music-making and birds has a wide and long history around the world. The fifth Dalai Lama, for example, composed a song entitled 'The Flying of the Cranes.' The length of the history is indicated by the fact that one of the earliest surviving pieces of music in Britain is the thirteenth-century song 'Summer is icumen in,' written down by the monk who kept the records at Reading Abbey, in which the song of the cuckoo is emulated.

The motif of the cuckoo's call was subsequently often employed by composers. Handel, for example, coupled it with the nightingale's song. Advances in sound technology have now led to the use of actual birdsong in live concerts.

The history of the musical connection includes, among many others, the following works:

1 William Byrd, aptly named, wrote songs about hawks in the seventeenth century.

2 Igor Stravinsky wrote a ballet called *The Firebird*, first produced in Paris in 1910.

3 Stravinsky based his 1914 opera *Le Rossignol* on the story about the nightingale by Hans Christian Andersen.

4 Mozart's *The Magic Flute* has a bird catcher called Papageno who plays his pipes to imitate and attract birds.

5 Beethoven incorporated the calls of the nightingale, the quail, and the cuckoo into his *Pastoral Symphony*.

6 Wagner, in *Lohengrin*, had his hero, the Knight of the Grail, arrive on a skiff drawn by a swan.

7 Sibelius uses a Finnish legend in his orchestral tone poem 'The Swan of Tuonela.'

8 Nikolay Rimsky-Korsakov's opera *The Golden Cockerel* was banned in Russia because it was considered to be seditious. The magic cockerel crowed whenever the kingdom was in danger. It was first performed in St. Petersburg in 1909, the year after the composer's death.

9 Janáček's opera *The Cunning Little Vixen* was first performed in 1924. It included a cockerel, a hen, and a hen chorus, a Screech Owl, and a woodpecker.

10 In 1914 Ralph Vaughan Williams composed an evocation of summer in his *The Lark Ascending*.

11 Olivier Messiaen was not only a devout Christian but also a keen ornithologist. His opera *Saint Francis of Assisi* includes a scene of the saint preaching to the birds. His *Catalogue d'oiseaux* is a work of 13 piano pieces based on 13 birds from different regions of France. His *Reveille des Oiseaux* is an orchestral work derived from avian sources.

Messiaen once confessed that birdsong for him was a refuge 'in my darkest hours, when my uselessness is revealed to me.'

12 Maurice Ravel drew on birdsong in his orchestral works, song cycles, and in small-scale pieces like *Oiseaux Tristes* for solo piano.

13 In Frederick Ashton's blissful ballet *La Fille Mal Gardée*, there is a dance for a rooster and four hens.

Heavenly Music

But the Nightingale, another of my airy creatures, breathes
such sweet loud musick out of her little instrumental throat,
that it might make mankind to think miracles are not
ceased. He that at midnight, when the very labourer sleeps
securely, should hear, as I have very often, the clear airs, the
sweet descants, the natural rising and falling, the doubling
and redoubling of her voice, might well be lifted above the
earth, and say, 'Lord, what music hast thou provided for
the Saints in Heaven, when thou affordest bad men such
musick on Earth!'

The Compleat Angler by Izaak Walton (1593–1683)

The Intention of God

I listen with reverence to the birdsong cascading
At dawn from the oasis, for it seems to me
There is no better evidence of the existence of God
Than in the bird that sings, though it knows not why,
From a spring of untrammeled joy that wells up in its heart.
Therefore I pray that no sky-hurled hawk may come
   plummeting down,
To silence the singer, and disrupt the Song.
That rhapsodic, assured, transcending song
Which foretells and proclaims, when the Plan is worked out,
Life's destiny: the joyous, benign Intention of God.

A poem originally written in Arabic, source unknown

Index

Accipitridae, 47
Achelaus, 41
Adam, 75, 103
Aeschylus, 44, 45, 112
Aesop, 69
Africa, 7, 17, 61, 62, 88, 185
Alaska, 48, 99
Alcedines, 83
Alcuin of Tours, abbot, 193
Alcyone, 85
Aldhelm, saint, 196
Alexander the Great, 40, 108, 109
Alfred the Great, king, 53
Ammon, 26
Anatidae, 66
Ancrene Wisse, 122
Andersen, Hans Christian, 166, 198, 199, 200
Andrews, Solomon, 47
Antony of Egypt, saint, 139
Aphrodite, see Venus
Apollo, 1, 9, 52, 117, 162, 165
Aquinas, Thomas, xiv, 130
Arabia/Arab, 53, 201; Arab countries, 61
Arabian Nights, 39
Arctic, 66, 71, 82, 98
Argus, 112
Aristophanes, x, 21
Aristotle, 44
Arnold, Matthew, 193
Artemis, 117
Asclepius, 1, 2
Asia, 31, 96, 173
Athena, 96, 97
Atlantic, 129, 163, 173
Attila the Hun, 52
Aubrey, John, 29
Audubon, John James, 32, 47, 123, 183–186
Audubon Society, 132, 186
Augustine of Hippo, saint, 113, 114, 125
Augustus, 40
Austin, William, 9
Australia, 98, 167, 179, 185
Aztecs, 37

Baltimore Oriole, 189
Barnes, Juliana, 54, 55

Bartas, Guillaume du, 126
Basil the Great, saint, 85
Beethoven, Ludwig van, 200
Bell, J. G., 185
Beowulf, 164
Bernini, 29
Bestiarum/Bestiary, 126, 133
Bewick, Thomas, 53, 184
Bible, 30, 34, 42, 74, 75, 79, 92, 97, 103, 108, 138, 139
Bird features: beak, 14, 37, 44, 84, 87, 114, 130, 131, 143, 150, 167, 168; breeding/mating, 18, 70, 108, 110, 123, 125, 154, 157, 169, 170, 174, 180; cheeping, 26; claws, 13, 33, 50, 58; cooing, 25; eating/feeding, 10, 13, 50, 55, 62, 66-67, 83, 84, 92, 93, 107, 108, 122, 123, 124, 137, 157, 158, 174; egg, 12, 13, 14, 27, 45, 61, 69, 71, 81, 85, 89, 90, 108, 110, 123, 157, 159, 162, 169, 174, 180, 190; eye color, 50; eyes/eyesight, 37, 42, 43, 50, 51, 88, 95, 99, 100, 144; feathers/plumage, 2, 3, 33, 43, 66, 77, 78, 85, 88, 89, 99, 100, 105, 107, 108, 109, 114, 119, 122, 123, 125, 130, 148, 168, 170, 174, 175, 180; feet/legs, 66, 70, 80, 87, 88, 116, 121; fighting, 3, 5-6, 146, 190; fishing, 99, 125; flight/flying, xi, 5-6, 50, 56, 63, 67, 87, 95, 105, 122, 123, 124, 161, 162, 173, 174; hearing/ears, 99, 100; molt/molting, 43, 66, 168; nest/nesting, xi, 12, 13, 14, 27, 61, 62, 85, 95, 122, 123, 130, 148, 149, 154, 157, 158, 174, 178, 179, 180; plumage color, 55, 83, 84, 85, 93, 107, 108, 109, 116, 122, 125, 135, 143, 150, 166, 167, 174, 177, 189; sacrifice, 1, 26, 28, 111; song/singing, 2, 4, 14, 17, 18, 31, 34, 103, 163, 164, 165, 174, 177, 179, 191-201; sound, 1, 12, 17, 88, 95, 98, 108, 113, 116, 154, 164; swimming, 66, 121, 122; tail, 2, 50, 107, 119; taming, 144; wings, 33, 50, 51, 56, 66, 78, 105, 123, 128, 142, 164, 168, 174
Black Prince, 89
Blackbird, xi

Blake, William, 38, 120, 148, 149, 177
Bluebird, 121, 153; Eastern Bluebird, 187; Mountain Bluebird, 187
Bobolink, 134
Bower Bird, 157
Britain, 6, 17, 19, 41, 44, 45, 53, 61, 79, 102, 133, 136, 142, 144, 148, 163, 167, 168, 176, 177, 182, 186, 199
Browne, Thomas, 44, 165
Browning, Robert, xv, 191
Buddhism/Buddhist, 109, 111
Buffon, comte de, 181
Bunyan, John, 187
Burnett, Frances Hodgson, 144
Burton, Richard, 87
Byrd, William II, 47
Byron, lord, 117

Caesar, Julius, 70, 102, 138
Caitlin, George, 34
California, 68, 128
Calvert, George, lord Baltimore, 189
Cambrensis, Giraldus, 71
Campion, Edmund, 71
Canada, 48, 82, 122
Canary, 108, 129
Canterbury Tales, 26, 169
Cardinal, 121, 187, 189
Carnan, Thomas, 74
Carroll, Lewis, 135
Carson, Rachel, 124
Cartier, Jacques, 32
Cassin, John, 154
Cat, 3, 58, 73, 98, 108, 158
Catesby, Mark, 182, 183
Celtic, 40, 70, 181
Central America, 12, 37, 84
Cerealia, 16
Ceres, 16
Cervantes, 55
Ceyx, 85
Chanticleer, 6-7
Charlemagne, 41, 73, 193
Charles I, king, 29, 113, 169
Charles, prince of Wales, 89
Chaucer, Geoffrey, 7, 26, 58, 79, 102, 157, 169, 196
Chester, Robert, 117
Chicago, 62
Chicken, 2, 77, 107, 190
China/Chinese, 10, 34, 46, 53, 68, 88, 101, 111, 159, 198
Christianity/Christian, xii, 5, 32, 33, 42, 43, 44, 97, 103, 112, 113, 114, 116, 125, 139, 150, 178, 200
Cicero, 137, 138
Circe, 52
Clark, Andrew, reverend, 146
Clark, William, 34, 189
Coat of arms/heraldry, xii, 130, 144, 166, 167, 168, 189

Cock, 1-10, 45, 157, 159, 179
Coleridge, Samuel Taylor, xvi, 165, 166, 193
Columba, saint, xi
Congreve, William, 128
Cooper, James Fenimore, 50
Coraciiformes, 83
Cormorant, 121, 129
Coverdale, Miles, 75
Coward, Noel, 82
Cowper, William, 155
Cromwell, Oliver, 178
Crow, 8, 61, 96, 135, 136, 142
Crusade, 41, 54; Third Crusade, 167
Cuckoo, 11-23, 176; Black- and Yellow-billed, 12; cuckoo clock and birdcage clock, 20; cuckoo spit, 21; European Cuckoo, 12; Hawk Cuckoo, 12; Squirrel Cuckoo, 12
Cupid, 157

Dalai Lama, 199
Dante, Alighieri, 126
Darwin, Charles, 185
David, 42
David, Elizabeth, 77
Decimus, Brutus, 30
Degas, Edgar, 122
Dickens, Charles, 82, 140
Diodorus, Siculus, 102
Dionysus, 179
Donne, John, 144
Douglas, Norman, 77
Dove, xii, 25-36, 50, 52, 84, 176, 193; Turtle Dove, 27, 31, 34, 35
Drake, Fancis, 129, 163
Drayton, Michael, 79, 147
Duck, 66, 123
Dunnock, 14

Eagle, 37-48, 49, 50, 130, 176, 187; African Crowned Eagle, 38; Bald Eagle, 46, 47, 48, 133; Giant Eagle, 39; Golden Eagle, 38, 46; Harpy Eagle, 37; Rukh, 39; Washington Eagle, 47
Eagle Dance, 40
Easter Egg, 90
Eating birds, 75, 76, 77, 80, 114, 131, 148, 169, 170, 190, 197, 198
Edward I, king, 168
Edward III, king, 44, 54, 89
Edward VII, king, 170
Edwards, George, 181, 182
Egypt/Egyptian, xii, 26, 27, 51, 52, 53, 69, 70, 88, 90, 102, 125, 133, 181, 184
El Greco, 32
El Hamam del Aroussa, 27
Elijah, 139
Eliot, George (Mary Ann Evans), 7, 152
Elizabeth, queen, 76
Elizabeth II, queen, 54
England (see also Britain), 3, 13, 16, 17, 57,

65, 72, 74, 79, 80, 81, 96, 97, 114, 118, 129, 131, 143, 153, 166, 178, 184, 189
Ennead, 69
Europe/European, 7, 13, 15, 40, 41, 50, 53, 61, 77, 121, 143, 146, 148, 151, 157, 167, 168, 176, 181, 185, 186;
  Northern Europe, 96, 135
Eustathius, saint, 100
Eve, 75, 103

Falcon, 37, 49–64, 187; Gyrfalcon, 54; Kestrel, 55, 62; Hobby Falcon, 55, 60
Falconiformes, 37, 49, 50
Felix, brother, 196, 197
Flamingo, 123
Fleet, Thomas, 74
Fokine, 171
Fowl, 3, 10, 71, 169, 190
Foxe, John, 4
Foxe, Richard, bishop, 130
France/French, 3, 5, 6, 16, 19, 53, 54, 70, 73, 76, 77, 81, 142, 148, 155, 173, 176, 178, 181, 200
Francis of Assisi, saint, xi, xii, 156, 200
Franklin, Benjamin, 46, 47, 184
Frederick II of Brandenburg, 168
Frederick II of Hohenstaufen, emperor, 58
Freemasonry, 127
French Revolution, 3, 30
Froissart, 54

Gabriel, archangel, 70
Galliformes, 107
Gannet, 121
Ganymede, 39, 40
Garuda, 38
Gay, John, 96
Genghis Khan, 30, 53, 99
George I, king, 73
George IV, king, 184
Germany/Germans, 20, 41, 59, 62, 74, 78, 105, 125, 148, 155, 169, 171, 196
Geronimo, 101
Gerrard, John, 71
Gertrude, saint, 125
Gibbons, Orlando, 164
Gilby, Anthony, 75
Goldfinch, xii, 148, 175
Goldsmith, Oliver, 81
Goodwood House, 181
Goose, xi, 8, 55, 65-82, 169; Barnacle Goose, 70, 71; Bean Goose 67; Brant/Brent (Brown) Goose, 65, 66, 67; Canada Goose, 66; Chinese Goose 66; goose bumps, 81; goose fair, 80; goose game, 81; Greylag Goose, 66; Mother Goose 73, 74; Sea Goose/Merganser 66; Snow Goose, 82; Stubble/Lag/Lea Goose 67; Swan Goose, 66; Ware Goose, 67
Goose Bible, 75
Gosse, Edmund, 193

Gould, John, 184,185
Gray, Thomas, 104
Greece/Greek, 1, 5, 16, 39, 69, 76, 77, 88, 93, 97, 108, 109, 162, 174, 197
Gregory of Nyssa, saint, 33
Gregory the Great, saint, 91, 92
Griffiths, Bede, xvi
Grimm, brothers, 177
Gull, 124; Laughing Gull, 125; Western Gull, 129; California Gull, 189; Seagull, 190
Gwylym, David Ap, 194, 195

Hamlet, 4, 58, 101, 127
Handel, 199
Harold, king, 54
Harrier, 50
Hawk, 29, 37, 47, 49, 50, 51, 57, 58, 187;
  Cooper's Hawk, 50; Goshawk, 55;
  Northern Goshawk, 50;
  Sharp-shinned Hawk, 50; Sparrow Hawk, 54, 61, 62, 160
Hebrew, 1, 12, 42, 122, 139
Hen, 6, 7, 8, 10, 89, 118, 157, 174, 200; Blue Hen, 190; Rhode Island Red Hen, 190
Henry II, king, 53, 169
Henry VII, king, 169
Henry VIII, king, 57, 126
Hera/Juno, 16, 69, 112, 113
Hermes, 93, 112
Hermit Thrush, 190
Herod, king, 41
Heron, xi, 58; Black-crowned Night Heron, 129
Herrick, Robert, 148
Hesiod, 16
Hilda of Whitby, saint, 75
Hindu/Hinduism, 27, 38, 69, 109, 111
Holy Spirit, xii, 32, 52
Homer, 52, 163
Hood, Robin, 147
Hopkins, Gerard Manley, 63, 64, 86, 110
Horus, 51, 52, 88
Hosking, Eric, 103
Housman, A. E., 17
Hugh of Saint Victor, 34
Hugh, saint, xi, 167
Hummingbird, 183, 185

Ibis, 52
Icarus, 93
Ice Age 173
Illustrators of birds, 181-186
Incas, 52, 99
India, 3, 12, 31, 39, 53, 69, 88, 108, 109, 111, 118, 136
Indonesia/Indonesian, 3, 31, 84
Innocent III, pope, 71
Inuit, 98
Io, 112
Ireland, 54, 71, 138, 166, 178
Isaiah, 42

Isidore, saint, 125
Israel, 47; Lake of Galilee, xi
Italy/Italian, xi, 5, 32, 61, 75, 82

James the Greater, apostle and saint, 7
James, king, 5
Japan, 53, 99
Jay, 134, 135
Jefferson, Thomas, 183, 189
Jerome, saint, 97, 126, 139
Jesus Christ, xiv, 8, 28, 33, 35, 40, 43, 52, 90,
    100, 101, 103, 113, 114, 125, 126, 127,
    133, 150, 159, 178, 196
'Jim Crow,' 140, 141
John, king, 19, 53
Johnson, Samuel, 81
Jonson, Ben, 60, 163
Joseph, 28
Josephine, empress, 167
Judaism, 2, 12, 27, 28, 34, 77, 90, 92
Juno, see Hera
Jupiter, see Zeus

Kansas, 129, 185
Keats, John, 101, 191, 193
Kentigern, saint, xi, 144
Kestrel, 55, 62, 63
Ketterer, Franz Anton, 20
Kevin, saint, xi
Kingfisher, 83-86; Belted Kingfisher, 83;
    Halcyon, 84, 85, 86; Kookaburra, 84;
    Mountain Yellow-billed Kingfisher, 84;
    Oriental Dwarf Kingfisher, 84; Paradise
    Kingfisher, 84; Ruddy Kingfisher, 84;
    Shovel-billed Kingfisher, 83
Kite, 47, 50
Kublai Khan, 53

Lark, 55, 156
Latin, xi, 3, 8, 41, 47, 50, 60, 64, 72, 73, 75,
    81, 96, 97, 130, 158, 162, 176
Lear, Edward, 98
Ledwidge, Francis, 156
Leto, 116, 117
Leviticus, 28, 122
Lewis, Meriwether, 34, 189
Leyland, Frederick R., 119
Lilford, lord, 96
Lilith, 103
Lincoln, Abraham, 190
Linne, Carl von, 88
Longfellow, Henry, 196, 197
Lorenz, Konrad, 67
Louis XV, king, 181
Lyly, John, 157

Magpie, 135
Mallard, 169
Malo, saint, xi, 179
Manlius, Marcus, 79
Marius, 40

Marlowe, Christopher, 137
Martin of Tours, saint, 75, 76
Marvell, Andrew, 193
Mary II, queen, 145
Meadow Pipit, 14
Medici, 81, 119
Mehemet Ali, pasha, 184
Mendelssohn, Felix, 25
Mercury, 2
Merlin, 54, 55
Mexico, 41, 82, 114
Middle Ages/Medieval, x, 3, 6, 7, 33, 41, 54,
    70, 90, 105, 125, 126, 133, 158
Migration, 15, 61, 122, 127, 164, 167
Militiades, 5
Milne, A. A., 98
Milton, John, 2, 43, 192
Minerva, 97
More, Thomas, 90
Mormons, 189
Morris, William, 118
Moses, 47
Mozart, Wolfgang Amadeus, 71, 200
Mughal, 115, 116, 118
Muslim, 2, 7, 109
Musset, Alfred de, 128

Napoleon, 41, 81, 167, 185
Nashe, John, 71
Native Americans/American Indians, 34, 40,
    68, 69, 138; Apache, 101; Canadian Indian,
    101; Pawnee Indians, 173, Hopi, 99
Nefermaat, 69
Neptune, see Poseidon
Newbery, John, 74
New York City, 62, 122, 132, 185
Nightingale, 1-8, 64, 108, 121, 148, 193,
    194, 195-201
Nightingale, Florence, 97
Niobe, queen, 116
Noah, 27, 30, 84, 139
Norse, 2, 5, 69, 135, 163
North America, 11, 46, 47, 50, 66, 74, 79,
    82, 83, 84, 99, 123, 132, 134, 173, 181,
    182, 183, 184, 185, 190
Northern Ireland (see also Britain), 30, 45
Nuruddin, sultan, 30

Obadiah, 42
Oceanus/Aeolus, 85
Odin, 135
Odysseus, 52, 76, 177
Ophelia, 101
Orpheus, 197
Osprey, 46, 50, 134
Ostrich, 87-93
Ovid, 81, 112, 195
Owl, 8, 12, 50, 95-106, 140; Barn Owl, 96,
    104; Brown Owl, 98; Burrowing Owl, 99;
    Eagle Owl, 105; Elf Owl, 96; Fish Owl,
    99; Great Gray Owl, 96; Great Horned

Owl, 96, 99; Little Owl, 96, 97; Screech Owl, 104; Tawny Owl, 103; Typical Owl, 96

Pacific, 30, 84
Pacific Northwest, 138
Palestine, 42, 108
Parsival, 168
Parthenon, 97
Partlet/Pertelote, 6
Passeriformes, 192
Paul the Hermit, saint, 139
Paul, saint, 163
Pavlova, Anna, 171
Peacock/peafowl, xii, 107-120, 169, 175; Burmese Green, 107; Common Blue, 108; Indian, 107, 108
Peale, Titian, 185
Pecham, John, 195, 196
Pelecanidae, 121
Pelecaniformes, 124
Pelican, 121-134; American White Pelican, 122; Brown Pelican, 122, 124, 132, 133
Pelican Island, 132
Penelope, 76
Penguin, 123
Pennant, Thomas, 164
Pepin the Short, 73
Pepys, Samuel, 29
Peregrine, 51, 54, 59, 61, 62
Perrault, Charles, 73
Perseus, 93
Persia/Persian, 5, 53, 108, 116, 118
Peter, saint, xi, 4, 5
Peterson, Roger, 186
Pheasant, 169; Chinese Golden Pheasant, 108; Himalayan Monal Pheasant, 108
Philadelphia, 74, 183, 185
Philo, 90
Philomel, 195
Picasso, Pablo, 25
Pigeon, 25-32, 55, 57, 61, 106, 169; Rock Pigeon, 26; Passenger Pigeon, 31, 57; carrier pigeon, 30, 61
Pike, Nicolas, 153
Pilgrim Fathers, 47, 143
Pius II, pope, 71
Plato, 165
Plautus, 19
Pliny, 10, 40, 114
Pliny the Elder, 30
Plutarch, 138
Pluto, 16
Poe, Edgar Allan, 140
Polycarp, saint, 33
Poseidon/Neptune, 162
Potter, Beatrix, 98
Primeval Egg, 69, 90
Prior, Matthew, 20
Prometheus, 39
Proserpina, 16

Purcell, Henry, 145

Quail, 47, 134, 169, 200
Queensbury, marquess, 80

Ra, 51
Rabbit, 55
Rameses II, 26
Raven, 135-142, 187
Ray, John, 181
Reed Warbler, 14
Reformation, 33, 72, 97, 127
Rembrandt, 40
Renaissance, 39, 58, 81, 102, 112, 185
Revolutionary War, 190
Rhea, 27
Rice, Thomas Dartmouth, 141
Richard the Lionheart, 167
Roadrunner, 11
Robert of Avenel, 54
Robin, xi, 143-152, 174; American Robin, 143; European Robin, 144, 145, 148, 149, 175
Roc, 39
Roman de Renart, 7
Rome/Romans, xii, 1, 2, 5, 10, 16, 19, 40, 41, 76, 79, 102, 108, 114, 137, 163, 195, 197
Rook, 135, 193
Roosevelt, Theodore, 132, 185
Rossetti, Christina, 193
Rossetti, Dante Gabriel, 118
Rostand, Edmond, 7
Rubens, Peter Paul, 113
Ruskin, John, 109
Russia, 41, 141, 163, 167, 170, 200

Sa'id, 116
Saint-Saëns, Charles Camille, 172
Salt Lake City, 190
Sampson, Thomas, 75
San Francisco, 128
Sand, George, 70
Satan, 126
Saul, king, 42
Scarlet Tanager, 134
Schulenberg, madame, 73
Scotland (see also Britain), 6, 16, 45, 71
Scott, Walter, 184
Servan, saint, 144
Seven Deadly Sins, 118, 119
Shag, 121
Shah Jahan, 53
Shakespeare, William, 4, 8, 19, 27, 43, 46, 49, 56, 58, 59, 73, 93, 101, 102, 103, 116, 127, 137, 147, 157, 163, 164
Shelley, Percy Bysshe, 38, 117
Sibelius, Jean, 200
Silesius, Angelus, 43, 127
Simpson, Edith, 11
Sinbad, 39

Sir Orfeo, 53
Skelton, John, 92, 93, 127, 158
Sloane, Hans, 182
Snake/rattlesnake/serpent, 11, 38, 39, 84, 92, 111, 126
Socrates, 2, 196
Solomon, king, 108
Song of Solomon, 27, 34, 35
South America, 37, 84, 99, 170
Southey, Robert, 89
Spain, 7, 61, 90, 103
Sparrow, 62, 133, 153-160, 174, 176; American Sparrow, 153; Cassin's Sparrow, 154; Chipping Sparrow, 154; English Sparrow, 153; Eurasian Tree Sparrow, 153; Hawk Sparrow, 160; House Sparrow, 153, 154, 155; Old World Sparrow, 153; Song Sparrow, 154; Vesper Sparrow, 154
Spencer, Lady Diana, 89, 169
Spencer, lord, 169
Spenser, Edmund, 43, 55, 73, 102, 162
Stanley, family, 44
Stephen, saint, 178
Stormy Petrel, xi
Straparola, Giovanni, 73
Stravinsky, Igor, 200
Strigiformes, 50, 95
Stroud, Robert, 129
Stubbs, John Heath, 27
Sufism/Sufis, 115, 141, 194
Swan, xi, 26, 66, 70, 161-172, 184; Bewick, 163, 164, 170; Black Swan, 171; Black Necked Swan, 170; Mute Swan, 163, 164, 167, 168; Trumpeter Swan, 170; Whistling Swan, 170; Whooper, 163, 164, 167; White Swan, 162, 166, 171

Talmud, 2
Tchaikovsky, 171
Tennyson, Alfred Lord, 37, 83, 193
Texas, 106
Thailand, 31
Thomas Aquinas, saint, xiv, 130
Thomas, Isaiah, 74
Thomson, Joseph, 87
Thoth, 52
Thunderbird, 40
Tiepolo, Giambattista, 32
Tintoretto, Jacopo Robusti, 113
Traherne, Thomas, 133
Tree Swallows, 153
Trogolytidae, 177
Tudor, Mary, 74
Tura, Cosima, 97
Turdidae, 143
Turkey, 80, 114; Wild Turkey, 46

Turnbull, E. Lucia, 14
Tutankhamun, 52
Tyndale, William, 75

United States (see also North America), 46, 66, 74, 82, 121, 122, 129, 131, 148, 186, 189
Uraeus, 52
Urban IV, pope, 130

Venus/Aphrodite, 27, 69
Victoria, queen, 62
Vincent of Saragossa, saint, 139
Vinci, Leonardo da, 93
Virgil, 163
Virgin Mary, xi, 15, 28, 32, 33, 72
Vulture, xii, 12, 37, 42, 47, 136

Wagner, Richard, 168, 200
Wales (see also Britain), 70, 146, 178
Walpole, Horace, 131
Walton, Izaak, 201
Washington, DC, 185
Weathercock, 4-5
Webster, John, 147
Wellington, duke, 30, 62
Werburga, saint, xi, 75
Western Meadowlark, 189
Wharton, Edith, 128
Whistler, James McNeill, 119
White, Gilbert, reverend, 104, 105, 108, 110, 140, 192
White Sully, 3
Whitman, Walt, 190, 191
Whittingham, William, 75
Willoughby, Francis, 181
Wilson, Alexander, 183, 185
Wodin, 69
Woodcock, 18, 169
Woodpecker, 96, 131, 193, 200
Wordsworth, William, xv, 23, 143, 161, 166, 193
World War I, 30
World War II, 30, 61, 133
Wren, xi, 173-180, 184, 192; Cactus Wren, 179; Canyon Wren, 179; European Wren, 173; Fairy Wren, 179; Goldcrest, 177; Winter Wren, 173; Rock Wren, 180
Wright brothers, 93

Yeats, W. B., 111, 116, 155, 166
Yellowstone National Park, 170

Zenodotus, 146
Zeus/Jupiter, 16, 39, 40, 85, 112, 162

Acknowledgments

Many people have contributed consciously or unconsciously to the writing of this book, and we want to warmly thank them all but without naming individuals and thereby, inevitably, leaving out some who deserve mention.

However we owe an especial thanks to two individuals in particular. Firstly to Erica Hughes whose initial researches were invaluable to us and formed the basis of our own writing. Secondly, to Jan Spurlock Stockland whose editing skills transformed the text and whose all-round contribution was of paramount importance.

A special thanks goes to Alec Hodson, a colleague from Able Types and a bird lover, for his many stories. And another very special thanks to Eleesha Allen, goddaughter aged eleven at the time, who spotted Drake's ship's name.

Lastly, to Christine Smith and all at Canterbury Press for their encouragement and sound advice and for giving us the opportunity to share with the public our own fascination with and love of birds.

Scripture quotations are from:

New Revised Standard Version of the Bible, copyright 1989 by the Division of Christian Education of the National Council of the Churches of Christ in the USA. Used by permission. All rights reserved. Quotes from the NRSV are used on the following pages: xiv (twice), 27, 28, 32, 35, 37, 104, 154, 159.

Authorized Version of the Bible (The King James Bible), the rights in which are vested in the Crown, are reproduced by permission of the Crown's Patentee, Cambridge University Press. Quotes from the AV are used on the following pages: 5, 25, 34, 108, 138, 139.

Holy Bible, New International Version, copyright 1973 by International Bible Society. Used by permission. All rights reserved. Quotes from the NIV are used on the following pages: 42, 109.

The New English Bible with the Apocrypha, copyright 1961 by the Delegates of the Oxford University Press and the Syndics of the Cambridge University Press. Used by permission. All rights reserved. Quotes from the NEB are used on page 91 (twice).